Mitch

Drakken Brotherhood

Book 1

Mitch

Drakken Brotherhood

Book 1

Carol Shaughnessy

Paranormal Romance with Bite

ISBN: 978 1725743595

Cover Design:	Gina Dyer
Photography:	Georigana Fields
	Apopium/ Depositphoto.com
Editors:	Melba Moon, Mary Marvella
Interior Design:	Melba Moon

Chapter 1

Commander Mitchell "Mitch" Bolton stood at attention. He let nothing of his opinion show on his face or in his eyes. Inside he was a seething mass of anger, the kind of destructive anger he'd fought so long to contain and control.

"Yes, sir."

"I know you, Mitch. You don't like this." The general sighed and left the window where he'd been watching the antics of the new recruits on the parade ground.

"You're my oldest officer here. I trust your judgment. But this is bigger than either of us." When he took his seat the old leather covering the chair squeaked as the chair groaned with the added weight.

"I need eyes on the inside, a mind that knows what to look for and how to interpret the information." Clasping his hands together, the general missed nothing in his commander's stance.

"Yes, sir," Mitch repeated, hardly willing to accept orders that sounded as if they were generated from any one of a hundred science fiction novels or movies, for that matter. It was a story old as the military. It resulted from some overpaid brain wanting to help the defense fund by creating super soldiers, maybe even robotic ones.

"Permission to speak freely." Even knowing they were alone, Mitch still hesitated making the request. The general wasn't going to like his two cents worth, but Mitch couldn't hold back.

"Granted." As soon as the softly spoken word left his mouth, he leaned back in his chair as Mitch leaned forward, planting both hands on the desk.

Teeth bared in a hard sneer, he looked at his commanding officer. "You seriously believe this trial will go into effect? That somehow, through folklore interpreted by a woman and a serum from a recipe book printed on bark, it will turn men into organic berserkers?" Mitch's voice remained a low growl, as if he wanted no one to hear the unreality he clearly outlined. He pulled his hands back, taking a step away from the broad divide between them. Body aching to move, he stilled every nerve, watching silently, grasping for control. If he let it all out he'd likely be facing jail time. It was imperative he clamp down on that need for action, at least until he cooled down and agreed to this impossible mission.

He took a cautious step and then another, feeling the rage disperse though his feet. Calming, he slowed his pacing and took several deep breaths. It was an old trick he'd picked up long ago, letting the anger drain away. It usually worked.

"I'm supposed to handpick a team of men from these volunteers who are to go underground and live." He raised his hand before the general could speak. He wanted no misunderstandings between them about this ridiculous assignment. "These men, every one, agreed to give their all, all of them Special Forces across all branches of the military, from SEALs to Raiders." The Marines finally reinstated their Special Forces group, giving it the same title as before it had been disbanded. MARSOCs finest and probably its youngest had been offered to the visionary project. Shaking his head, Mitch turned around to make another pass in front of the desk. "They volunteered for extra hazardous duty.

"I don't have issue with that. They signed on to fight and die for their country, but we plan to inject them with an untried serum and expose them to light studies that will determine how effective all of these "witchcraft potions" are at creating the perfect soldier." He ran his hand through hair that was already in need of a cut.

"I've been through some crazy schemes, but this takes the cake. Are you trying to poison us? Is this something on which we need to be wasting money and time? Hell, the man-hours and power waste alone boggles the mind. You do realize how futuristic this sounds?" He stopped the pacing he hadn't realized was moving him around the office.

"I know something about science fiction and this would be a box office flop." Mitch turned to face the desk and the man sitting behind it.

"I know how it sounds. This comes from very high." Unable to define the statement, the general sighed. "It isn't a choice. Not for me or for you." He pushed the innocent looking file toward Mitch.

"Here are the guidelines for picking the specific soldiers we're looking to recruit. Make sure all of them are volunteers looking forward to this mission. There is an abridged mission outline, also included there." He rounded the desk, moving to Mitch's side. The general met Mitch's level gaze as he slid over the thick file. "All we can do is our best to make sure this comes out good for all."

"Super soldiers based on Viking Berserkers." Voice filled with disdain with the very idea, Mitch looked down at the expandable file on the desk. The minute he reached for it he'd gave up the fight. There was no use fighting it. If Greg thought this was the best place for him, he'd be there. But he wanted Greg, as family and as his commanding officer, to know how badly intuition had dogged him since he'd heard the first rumor. He'd dismissed it as another scheme with no chance of gaining credibility. Unfortunately, the rumors proved true. The shadow that warned him of danger filled his head, standing firmly entrenched.

"I trust you to follow orders. Keep in touch with this office." Greg offered his hand. "Be safe."

Mitch hesitated, staring at his cousin. He took the offered hand and clasped it firmly in his.

"I'll see you." Greg pulled him close. Both men looked over their shoulders at thirty years of aging fading away quickly.

When they parted, Mitch held the information to his side. With a nod, he turned on his heel and left the office. Stomach tight, Greg watched him go. If the family trait ran true, this would not end well. Yet he had no choice. There were whispers of the lead scientist using military funds to perfect the process he'd kept secret. Once it was through testing and the specifics proven using the government dime, it was rumored the serum and the specific light wavelength that activated it would go to the highest bidder.

Greg rubbed the back of his neck, strain in the muscles keeping it tight. He returned to watching the new recruits, his mind far away. While he'd been raised knowing the story of the family's unique genetic makeup, his uncle, Mitch's father, had kept the secret away from his family.

Their bodies carried a strain of DNA not present in most other humans. It allowed them to age gracefully, to keep their incredible mental acuity well past human norms. Their bodies rejected viruses and bacteria, so they were never sick. A movement below, close to the building, caught his gaze. Greg sighed, glancing down as he watched Mitch stride angrily to the parked car. He wanted to let his cousin in on the secrets. There had been so many times he'd wanted to let Mitch know as boys. He'd never managed to break the silence about the forbidden topic.

A fine soldier, Greg finally managed to get Mitch stationed under him on the base, after the first notices of this new mission spec crossed his desk. With a sigh, he turned to sit at the desk, the weight of his orders weighing heavily on his shoulders. When he understood what might happen, Mitch was the logical choice. It would mean that Mitch was walking into this blind to his nature, but that very nature would be the one thing that would keep him alive. Of that, Greg had no doubts.

Mitch already doubted the mission without even seeing the specs. When the full story of the trials was uncovered, either he'd go MIA or he'd buck every level of the mission hierarchy until he'd torn down the Pentagon. There were facets Greg doubted on this mission. Luck ran with him that the ones who'd chosen this task for him hadn't known he had an ace in Mitch Bolton.

The man was hell against anything but straight up soldiering, and it showed. He'd be a valuable asset.

Mitch jumped off the helicopter after he'd tossed his bag to the ground. He learned to travel light long ago. Dust puffed around his feet, sweet and choking as the whirling blades lifted it and he waved the chopper away. Letting the air settle around him, he shifted the backpack and shouldered the loaded sea bag. He took a moment to look around. Camouflaged by the clinging desert dust, the house was part of the wildness around it. Behind the house rose a butte, shading it for now. In the afternoon, the sun would clear the ridge and the house would be at the desert's hot mercy.

Across from the front door the desert rushed out like a carpet, every shade of brown from cream to umber wove together in an incredible display. In the distance rose a ridge, jagged and inhospitable looking. There was a line, crooked through the carpet, twin ruts that probably were a roadway. It led away into the distance, disappearing around the tail end of the ridgeback. A van waited by the front door. Must be someone leaving.

He moved to the door, pausing with his fist raised, and then simply reached for the knob. They had to be expecting him. And

8

according to the specs of this base, they had eyes on him the moment he landed.

Turning easily, he smiled at the implication of well-attended maintenance. The living room was homey and stuck in the seventies a good decade, long gone. A head peered around the door to the kitchen, he assumed, as the scent of fresh baked bread filled the air, replacing the dust in his lungs.

"You're new here."

"Smells good." Mitch stepped forward with a nod, slowing his next step when a 9mm eased into view. "I see." Holding his hands out, he dropped the bag. Moving slowly, he reached into his pocket for the billfold-sized packet he'd need to pass the guard. He tossed the packet to the feet of the baker. Never losing sight of Mitch, the male moved the packet past him with a booted foot.

"Please, come into the kitchen." The invitation was slow to come, but warm as the gun disappeared as quickly as it had appeared and as quietly.

"Mind if I catch my bag?"

"Of course, you'll need it."

Mitch complied, stomach growling at the scent.

"Butter?"

"I'm sorry?" Mitch asked and then turned into the room. A plate had been set with a slice of steaming bread.

"Would you like any butter on it? We have honey and peanut butter if you'd prefer."

"Honey is fine." Mitch dropped the bag in a free corner and accepted the bread, now generously topped with honey. The first bite was heaven, lost in the heat, texture, and sweetness, He didn't remember eating the rest. Another slice appeared.

"I am supposed to be here, we have the right-um-address?" While Mitch thoroughly enjoyed the treat, he wanted to make sure this was the actual base.

A chuckle stirred the air. "You are in the right place. It takes time to cycle personnel. They called ahead and there are folks who need a trip to town. We're waiting for them to come up and for their ride to get here. Then you load and down you go."

Mitch ate the second piece more slowly, enjoying every bite this time. That explained the van he'd seen outside. Their ride was here. He studied the team in the kitchen. The silent guard watched him closely without appearing obvious. The talkative one opened the oven and the smell of chocolate chip cookies surpassed the fresh hot bread.

"Tea or coffee?" He turned and asked Mitch.

"Coffee, black and hot." The talkative one of the pair poured the cup and brought it over to where Mitch had taken a seat at the table. The chrome and yellow Formica reminded him of his grandparent's house, of all things. Scarred by cups and plates slid across the surface, not to mention buffed by elbows, it was homey. Silence filled the ranch house. A soft purr of wind stroked the outside, giving only a whisper of sound.

Mitch's natural worry kicked in, goaded by the shadow of danger, a constant companion. His mind whirled with the past month as he sipped the strong brew. It had taken him that long to handpick the men who were to join him down here. They were to allow no women for their first run of serum and testing. Mitch didn't like it, hadn't grown any fonder of the mission, no matter how many times he'd read the file on the specifics. He'd swallowed his distaste and hoped for the best.

Every soldier, sailor, jarhead, guardie, and flyboy he'd picked should already be here, housed and getting adjusted to their specific world. Every amenity was included, meals, gym, pool. There was room down here for a basketball court. He hoped all were fine without sunlight. For the next twelve or so months, there would be little of that. His expected the stay would be no longer.

Mission parameters set out time lines for eighteen months, two years, and three years. Based on the success rate, there were added instructions for women once the males proved proficient to the purpose. He sighed. Why the fuck the military wanted berserker women he gave up trying to explain. There was no way he could make sense of that or condone it.

He snorted. Call him old fashioned or a chauvinistic throwback, Neanderthal even, he didn't think women needed to be front line fodder. With them rested the future of the world. He trusted they were strong and capable, resilient. Targets for enemy action? Not so much. He had to draw the line somewhere, so he could lay down his head and sleep at night.

They were giving up many things to participate in the trial. Not family, the men had no families, no children, and no ties. The orders were explicit on that point. Mitch's gut clenched. There was a better than even chance they would not return from these tests. That remained unspoken. Added to that, these men were in their sexual

10

prime and there were few women *Below*. The natives had already named their home, he'd found out from the chopper pilot.

He'd spent the night before with a woman he knew, but he wasn't attached to her. She'd been a good time, and he was just loose enough from the sexual Olympics that had lasted until he left her bed for the base. He'd dozed while waiting for the chopper, transportation from the last duty station to this one. A real nap, stretching out in a bunk, now his hunger had been sated, sounded like the best plan for the day. He had to report to the man leading the mission or testing as the civilians would have it. Then he had two days to settle in, make sure the roster was complete, and all would begin the testing, as long as no shit had hit the fan in the time he'd been out of contact traveling. There was always the chance something had gone wrong. How could it not? Given the insane logic trail for this whole venture, he didn't doubt trouble brewing for an instant. He set the empty cup on the table, still lost in thought.

He had a planner of things the men would need to do to keep busy. Too much testosterone, if not bled off, screamed trouble. The only alternative was to fill their days with tasks and their nights with exhausted slumber.

A grumbling noise, subliminal, brought him from the woolgathering. He looked around, trying to place the source of the growl. His host didn't seem to notice the vibration. Mitch stood, grabbing his backpack, guessing it was his ride.

"Head down the hallway. The end closet is the door." Like that, he'd been dismissed from the kitchen. The warmth of the previous conversation drained away. He shouldered his sea bag and stepped into the doorway of a bedroom to clear the hallway. Good thing, the door opened, and a woman's voice filled the house.

"Regina wanted me to get her some cheap stuff, but she works so hard. I think I'll go to the boutique in town and get her some really good scented soaps and shampoo." As full of life as the voice, the short curvy woman reflected every erg of that energy. She led the way from the elevator, a force of one, towing three very bemused males behind her. Mitch watched them down the hall, stepping to take his place, only to fall back when another woman left the elevator.

Tall and less curvy, she nodded as she passed him.

"I'm Amelia Jenkins, one of the bio techs."

"Commander Mitch Bolton." Neither reached out to clasp hands. Amelia nodded again, turning to follow the group into the day. Mitch

11

stepped into the elevator. The weight of his bag suddenly seemed too heavy to hold as the responsibilities on paper became flesh and blood.

Chapter 2

Regina piled the bags on her loveseat. She'd enjoyed shopping and loved the new highlights that turned her hair from dense deep auburn to intense streaks from brighter red to blond. Grabbing a drink from the kitchen, she settled in front of her computer. The desire for a nap pulled her toward the short hall and to her big bed, yet she wanted to check for results in the linguistic program she had running.

An urgent email caught her attention. She checked the sender, Dr. Emerson Laurel. Damn, she had to answer. If anyone on the face of the earth could derail her plans for the night, it would be the good doctor.

"Please," she begged whoever listened for swift prayers. "Let it be something simple."

The instructions were simple. She had to be packed and ready to leave by 0600 the day her travel reservations dictated, only three days from today. The missive also included instructions to begin the prescribed regiment of vitamins necessary for her successful integration into the controlled environment in which she'd be working. The shipment and instructions for their administration would be delivered the following day.

Lucky for her, she had no problem giving herself the stipulated injections. Still, Regina read the email several times before understanding the message. Her formulation of the serum, using archaic names for herbs and grasses, worked chemically. Regina hopped from the chair and danced around the room, cheering. She wished she had someone to share this with, thinking of her ex. At least he would be happy for her.

Their divorce was in part collateral damage. She worked with ancient manuscripts, translating them and then searching and sourcing ingredients called for to finish potions from ages ago. In another time she would be a druid because of the plant lore she memorized and used almost daily. Those intensive studies, most sending her around the world for long periods, created the sense of separation between the spouses. In time, it was easier to be roommates and then even that didn't work.

She sighed. The divorce was amicable and over. She went back to her computer, going through the email again.

This particular serum came from an archaeological dig in Norway. A newly discovered grimoire written in Old Norse runic script centuries old, falling apart with age, yielded this recipe for creating a berserker attack force. The last of the interpretation from a gnarly written tongue guaranteed increased strength, with the warning that a matching aggression manifested in the men taking the herbal mixture. Dr. Laurel was looking for monetary backing, already proposing the experiment to the military.

After delays in the translation, leading to misidentified ingredients, the formulation was finished a week ago, leaving her some free time while others took over the actual manufacture. Regina celebrated the success today, hence, her shopping spree for a new outfit and a new cut and color.

In the email Dr. Laurel outlined the next steps in the production and implementation of the serum. Beyond the animal testing, he had scheduled the human trials to begin in a few months.

Sure of her interpretation, she'd headed out on her pamper-me day. Now he'd confirmed it would do as the grimoire promised. Normally, this would be the last step for her, but for some reason Laurel wanted her by his side, assuring the future serum manufacture was perfect. She would also help with the injections and the clinical trials. She looked forward to it with a bit of trepidation. She was more comfortable with books than people, more cooperation and fewer attitudes. Guess that was about to change.

Her dancing over, she plopped out of breath into the chair, catching the edge of her desk and rolling back to finish reading the rest of the missive.

Also interested in the research, she wasn't surprised to see the military offering a secluded site, much bigger than the original one Laurel chose. This one seemed to be in the heart of the desert in Arizona. She had to be packed and ready to leave by 0600 the day her travel reservations.

Now that she had something to celebrate she could hardly wait until her favorite bar opened. Regina printed off the confirmation pages, sent back an acknowledgement of the email and a reserved thank you for the information. She sent the computer back to its linguistics program with a huge smile on her face. Success and recognition for her work at last. Her doctoral theses now completed, it only remained for her to finish compiling the last of the experimental data and getting her paper to the powers that be.

Finally, proof her theory that ancient medicine and cures would work on today's people was in her hand. Millions of manmade medicines could exist beside hundreds of dollars of herbs and potions with few to no side effects. Herbs and natural ingredients left less damage on human organs like the liver and kidneys. That would allow relief for those who already suffered from issues of those organs.

Regina snagged the bags with her new purchases and went to her bedroom. She jumped into the middle of the king sized bed, tossing the bags to the foot. Her headache finally starting to ease, she turned off her brain, settled her body and actually fell asleep.

Three exhausting days later, Regina reached her destination. The plane ride, the chopper trip, the van driving through miles and miles of sand finally pulled up to a rambling ranch style building. There, her bags and goods came together close to a huge moving dolly. She did not have to move the labs, thank goodness. She simply had to find quarters and then find the labs available for their studies.

The house looked deserted, no matter what she knew to be true. She watched the van turn around and head back the way it came, leaving a dust trail in its wake. Sighing, she looked around, her mind already underground in the facility that was to be her home.

A second round of animal testing would begin day after tomorrow. She needed to be here to observe, another knowledgeable set of eyes on hand, Dr. Laurel told her over the phone. He'd called between flights to make sure she was following orders.

Not much time to settle in and learn her way around the complex, which she understood took up five full floors underground, with several off shoot tunnels for storage and goods. She'd tried to memorize the dossier on the complex on the trip here. There was so much on her mind it was impossible to make sense of it in any detailed manner. Somewhere down there was her bedroom and the bathroom. There was an efficiency apartment set aside for her, but right now she wanted a shower and a nap.

The overnight flight to the base started her morning early. Once at base, she'd been ferried to a commuter plane, empty except for an officer in beige she didn't know and who didn't introduce himself. He was sleeping before the plane lifted off. Late morning she landed at a public airport, and was escorted across to her gate by two armed MPs. Loaded, the flight was delayed by bad weather so she'd managed to nap away that wait. In the air and down again in another public airport, possibly Dallas/Fort Worth, she wasn't sure since they rushed her through it so quickly. Back in the air, she was up then down, a short ride to a base, loaded into a helicopter. It beat its way out of civilization, dropping her on the doorstep of the little ranch house.

With another heavy sigh, the fragrance of the desert filling her lungs, she started loading the dolly. She looked up as a couple of uniforms came from the house to help. They took over as a proficient team, quickly stacking her boxes on the dolly and piling her bags beside it. She got out of their way.

They looked like desert creatures, some strange humanoid sand people in the digitized desert camouflage. Kepis over their heads blocked the sun from the back of their necks, dark glasses covered their eyes. A bandana, strange looking and worn bunched around their necks, keep the sand from invading their lungs, much as it had invaded her clothing and body.

In no time her belongings were loaded up and heading into the building. A good thing, since her fair skin was starting to burn in the unforgiving sun of the desert. She shivered at the difference in temperature outside and inside. Her nipples peaked and rasped against the lace of her bra, in turn scratching against the cotton weave of her shirt. Trying to ignore the heightened sensitivity, she pulled the welcome file from her portfolio. Things tightened low in her body and she wished she'd taken advantage of the offer from a computer tech in the bar.

At least she wouldn't be feeling aroused by the simple brush of cotton on her body.

They came to a stop after traversing a hall. Double bi-fold doors hid a freight elevator. A woman watched them from the kitchen arch. A hiss and the doors opened. Regina followed her belongings into the cave-like interior. She waited while the soldier latched the door, pressing a button on his side of the car. Silent, the descent began. Removing their kepis, the soldiers tucked them into the back of their BDUs. Could the handsome, rugged, young men be her test subjects?

When Regina glanced at the papers in her hand another shiver ghosted along her shoulders. This contained a map of the facility, her quarter's assignment and other things pertaining to her job. She pulled the address sheet and handed it to the man who seemed to be leading this little trip. He took it, wiping a hand through his buzz cut. He glanced at it, his brown gaze straying only once to her breasts before handing it back to her with a nod.

"You're close to the techs you'll be working with. The military are in another hall, the doctor and his assistant are a level up."

"Thank you." Regina wondered why Laurel wasn't with them, but then guessed he had better quarters. It was his idea they were working on, rank and privilege and all that.

The freight elevator took them down levels she did not bother to count. The grind was slow and for the most part silent. Dry desert air settled around the trio. She knew she looked exactly like she felt, hot, sweaty, windblown, sunburned and hungry. Before she would be able to take care of most of that, she had to unpack. A shower would perk her up. After that she would find the labs. She hoped the cafeteria would be serving something to eat.

Low blood sugar, lack of sleep, the chill in the air after hours baking in the desert sun as she traveled here had her mind wandering down unfamiliar paths. Her body warmed between the finest specimens of the male sex she'd seen recently. Even if they didn't appear human, yet.

Neither looked the least bit hot or chilled, impervious to the sudden changes of temperature. Even after loading her things and trundling them through this warren, they appeared normal and collected. Those BDUs had to be heavy, their boots hot. She walked behind them, letting the passages slip past her. She looked at her slip-on mocs. It was such a good idea this morning, yesterday morning, hell she'd forgotten, but now they left her footsore and blistered. The concrete floors definitely did not help. She wished she had on the sneakers in her overnight bag. Oh well, in a few minutes, maybe.

Traffic diminished in the passage the longer they walked. It made sense. Less traffic meant a good night's sleep. She hoped to be tired enough to sleep, anyway. Now the situation was so exciting she didn't know if that would be possible. For the next ten to twelve months this would be her home. She knew there were other females here, soldiers, some operations personnel. Regina had not seen one *Below* though.

Being surrounded by the males reminded her of her one magical night. Maybe that was what had her hormones rising, pushing her libido into overdrive.

Her introduction to passion, thorough and intense, had her body reacting to the tactile memories created. The muscles she strained working so hard at pleasure had relaxed and healed. Walking down the corridor with two men, both of them credits to their sex, stirred her imagination away from the every day and opened the stage in her dreams.

She'd been introduced to all the volunteers through their files. By now, she could name most on sight. But their dossiers contained headshots, no body, and she wondered if all the volunteers were such beautiful representations of the male form. Lost to fantasy, she checked out of reality.

She watched herself step up to the sandy haired marine, slowly unfastening those buttons from his starched shirt, peeling away the military mask as she removed his uniform. His last name, embroidered on his chest, let her know he is Davidson. Her arms coaxed behind her, she wonders for a moment what is happening. Wait, his dark haired companion with skin the color of mocha, hands calloused but gentle, is doing the same for her. She glances down to watch his hands, his skin such a delightful contrast against her paleness, cup and lift the weight of her breasts, offering them to his buddy. His name badge reads Coakley.

"Ma'am, do you have your key?"

Regina snapped back to the here and now so fast her switch in attention popped in her ears. By his tone of voice, this was not the first time he asked her.

"Um, yeah." Head out of the bedroom, Regina scolded herself feeling the flush rush to the tips of her ears. She opened the folder and removed the card from its sleeve. She ignored the heat rising to her face, starting at her ears and moving down into her chest.

"Please slide it into the reader and program your six digit entry code at this time." Davidson stepped away from the locking mechanism allowing her to see the pad. If he noticed anything wrong with her, beyond her inattention, she hoped he blamed it on travel exhaustion.

Behind her, he exchanged glances with his cohort.

She had expected this and thankfully already had a sequence

18

memorized. Her face surely glowed from the naughty daydream of the seduction of these men. The door opened with a hiss. It moved ponderously, making her wonder why.

"The doors act as both entrances and bulkheads. The area is geologically stable and this compound was blasted through bedrock and cradled within, but the military never takes chances. You will have to give it time to respond to open and close." Coakley answered her unasked question, then he motioned her inside.

The lights came up slowly to full brightness when they entered. She noticed a galley kitchen with a small stove, sink and refrigerator and a bar, serving as the table, separating that from the living room. That room looked bigger than her last apartment. A hallway led her into a bedroom and bath combo as big as the other side of the hall. No windows, thank goodness she did not suffer from claustrophobia. If she needed a bit of air, the packet explained that an organized shopping trip left for the closest town every other week, in case she wanted food or other things.

The bed was a king, a tall king. Evidently space was not a premium so far underground. Her walls were dusky blue, floors and ceilings were ivory. Unfinished in the traditional sense of the word, they were not smooth, but had a stucco look to them.

The linens were dark blue, shades of navy. The bathroom, done in shades of ivory and gold, boasted a three showerhead shower, double sinks and more than adequate storage for her few toiletries. Twin chests and a walk in closet completed the bedroom with a floor to ceiling mirror so she could see herself before leaving the room. The hallway had more storage and a nook for her computer and workstation setup.

The living room contained a flat screen television and a selection of DVD's, which told her cable was probably out of the question. Disappointed, she coaxed herself into a sincere smile, until Coakley handed her a remote.

"Ma'am, we have satellite connection, you have over one hundred channels." He smiled at her, the first human expression on his face. "Thank goodness it never goes out." He proceeded to explain the controls to her as Davidson rolled in the dolly and started unloading onto the great room floor.

Regina moved to help, and as soon as the last box hit the floor the men turned and headed out the door. Coakley did something on this side of the room and the heavy door slid shut.

"Thank you." Regina told the empty room. She sighed and turned to look around her. As soon as she noticed the rugs on the floor, she slipped off her shoes and flexed her bare toes in the fibers. Moaning at the feeling, she enjoyed the hedonistic moment.

In time, she started picking boxes and moving them into their respective areas. Her clothes to the bedroom, toiletries to the bath, research to the hallway so she could stumble over it as she carted box after box to its unpacking point.

Finally she looked in the fridge and grabbed water, thankful someone had put in a few staples for her. On site, the cafeteria served the bulk of the meals. Still, it was nice to have a place for snacks and leftovers. Sighing, she collapsed into the overstuffed couch and propped up her legs. Now all she had to do was unpack, shower and find a bite to eat. Se settled into the embrace of the couch and dozed off, making lists of what she needed to do before bed.

Chapter 3

"Who is she?" Davidson asked Coakley.

"That's the doc who's gonna make us stronger," Coakley said. He'd read up on the research and volunteered, same as Davidson and all the others down here. Everyone volunteered to be the next gen soldier in the service. It was only a matter of time before they became the first wave of a newly engineered fighting force.

"She's fucking hot," Davidson murmured. He glanced at Coakley to see if he agreed.

"Damn straight." Coakley smiled. "Wanna know what she was thinking about when you asked her for her key, *three times*?" Coakley was a highly rated psychic. His telepathy had brought him to the attention of the R&D team. All of the volunteers were rated psi operators, had skills in all disciplines and worked side by side down here. Davidson happened to be telekinetic. He looked at Coakley, reading his enlarged pupils and flaring nostrils.

"Go ahead, thrill me."

"She was seducing both of us, man. She was taking off your clothes and I was taking off hers. The most beautiful breasts I have ever seen were nestled in the palms of my hands." He held his hands out as if holding her, gently moving his fingers along imaginary flesh.

"Hot damn, Navy," Davidson's voice sounded breathless since his own body started to react. He imagined the action now. He'd taken to the nickname for his buddy when they'd met on the bus ride out of town.

"No shit, Kenny. She was smoking hot and ready. Hell, I bet she's still ready to go." He looked over his shoulder as though considering a return trip to help the lady out. He was amazed at the clarity of her thoughts as Doc Regina daydreamed. Her peach nipples, the puckered areoles, her delight at his darker skin next to the paleness of hers, the rasp of her breathing while she dreamed appeared crystal clear to him. Man, if she was going to stay down here she would need shield work 24/7. If they wanted a volunteer for that chore, his hand would be first up.

"Let's get this dolly back and hit the chow line. We should be off duty in about thirty minutes." Kenny glanced back down the corridor, her quarters lost in the turns behind them. They would see her again.

Regina woke stiff. After dragging her tired body out of the embrace of the sofa, she did a few stretches as she looked around at her life stored in cardboard boxes stacked here and there. Twenty-seven boxes and three suitcases later, she tipped her head back as the hot water cascaded over her. Her stomach complained about the wait time, but Regina ignored it and reached for the soap.

Having three showerheads was a luxury she'd never experienced before, and for a moment she wondered how much those amenities cost the taxpayer. Feeling guilty, she rushed the shower so she could study the plans for her level she'd not managed to memorize. After she dressed she headed with confidence to the cafeteria, only to find herself wandering since she'd left the map lying on her bed.

"You look lost." A woman's chipper voice called out, stopping Regina from taking another wrong turn. "Unless you're looking for the men's quarters." The laughter in the voice made Regina smile as she turned.

"Guilty."

A plump woman approach her. "Thought so. They're at mess anyway, no one's there. Follow me." Blond frizzy hair sporting a yellow pencil bobbed as she turned back. Regina, not quite a head taller, gained her side.

"Regina Coombs."

"Heard you were going with Gardner now. You're the doctor who discovered the serum."

"I am." She followed the woman through corridors past her room. She'd answered both questions.

"Your quarters." Her guide pointed down the connecting hallway. "I'm Tracy, one of your assistants. If you come out of your quarters, turn right, follow the corridor until you reach that dim light, hang a left, you get food." Suiting actions to directions, Tracy led her to the cafeteria.

Once the door opened Regina's mouth watered. A conventional array of buffets meandered around the huge room. Arrangements of tables in every grouping, from pairings to round family sized tables seating eight or more, filled the room. Her guide, gone silent, drew her attention. Regina's gaze followed the stare and caught a soldier smiling at her. The man made a move to stand, only to settle at Tracy's sharp headshake.

"Problems?" A sigh told Regina there was a long story here.

"The mad scientist doesn't want any personal entanglements with *his* test subjects." Tracy started across the floor, heading for the trays of glasses and plates. Regina hurried to follow her. Obsessive with his test subjects, Dr. Laurel was capable of declaring them off limits. Smiling, Regina caught up to Tracy, adding a plate to a tray. They wandered around the food bars, each taking a bit here and there. Once their plates were full they headed by unspoken agreement to a table for two.

"The mad scientist?"

Already eating, Tracy nodded. "He picked up the nickname about a week ago. He stormed into the lab where we were preparing another batch of your recipe on some rant that the military, hand-chosen for these tests, were off limits to any personnel. We were not to address them at any time unless they were in the current testing phase. Our conversations would be limited to questions relevant to their processing."

Regina thought it over. It sounded like a power move to her. She liked the new nickname. It fit the control freak like a second skin "I arrived earlier today. I know he's a bit extreme in regards to this experiment. Maybe it was taken the wrong way." Regina tried to put a bit of oil on troubled waters.

"He's an ass. We know what we're doing. We know the parameters of this group's testing. We are professional."

Regina couldn't argue. He'd been her least favorite partner, always holding others up to a standard only he imagined. It wasn't a perfect world, never had been, never would be, yet he pushed hard to make it fit his mold.

Regina could see how enforced confinement would throw personalities together, especially here with no other outlet for the sexual needs of young, healthy males and females. There was no evidence that mixing would in any way affect the outcome of the trials. Here was a prime example. The soldier, if the green fatigues he wore was a true indication of his branch, was clearly focused on Tracy and she on him. The doctor in charge was denying them all for

23

a power play.

"So forget him for now. Care to bring me up to speed on where we are?" She couldn't solve this issue, not without extra information. Arriving today left her already behind the loop.

"We reproduce the serum daily, like I said, following your recipe. Always works, always comes out perfect. We store it. Dr. Laurel takes it, does his private research or experiments, whatever."

"How much are you producing?" She hadn't expected to hear that.

"If our source of product is stocked, we make five gallons. When we're short, only two or so."

"He takes all of it?"

Tracy nodded, glancing up as her soldier moved past her. She sighed, dropping her gaze to her plate. "Not sure where it goes, hell, he could be dumping it down the drain."

Regina shook her head. That wasn't like the meticulous scientist. But why would he be hoarding the serum?

"A three-month shelf life in temperatures between sixty and eighty degrees allows the serum to remain stable. After that the serum begins breaking down, losing the desired effects."

"We already know that. Have had some stored that long. In animal testing it loses about two percent effectiveness per month after that."

"How are we for ingredients?" Regina pushed her tray back, taking her water glass and sipping as she watched Tracy finish.

"Delivery received yesterday contained three months of everything we need." Tracy tipped her glass back, emptying it. "We have enough for over four hundred gallons. Now we're injecting the first team it doesn't stockpile." Regina sat up.

"I was told animal testing was continuing for at least a month longer."

"No, ma'am. We've been injecting the first team for ten days now."

Anger flushed the confusion from Regina's mind. The adrenalin surge surprised her, creating an ache where she'd been religiously following Laurel's instructions on her injections of vitamins. Now underground, she understood the need. She rubbed the side of her stomach, wishing she could choose another spot for a time.

Thinking about his lack of transparency, his singular decision to move forward at a faster pace, she bit her lip, knowing her features flushed with her emotions.

"We received a new timeline from the mad scientist and began on the men." Tracy, only then noticing Regina's fury, leaned close. "It is okay to begin with them, right? I mean—" She glanced out the door. "I know this team now. Don't tell me it's hurting them."

The alarm in her voice tore at Regina. For a moment she wondered if she'd ever experienced anything close to what Tracy had for her soldier. "No, of course not, they would have shown symptoms by now. The serum is safe, and it needs time to build into the human system. Don't worry. I'm sure your soldier is fine." Tracy's fair skin blushed. .

"He's not my soldier." Both women knew the lie as it left her lips. Regina smiled at the quick denial but didn't push it.

"I've studied all the animal testing. The serum doesn't linger long, remember," Regina assured the perky blond. At her nod, Regina gathered her tray.

"How easy is it going to be for me to get lost on the way to the lab tomorrow?"

Regaining her humor, putting her worry aside, Tracy stood. Her teeth stopped chewing her lower lip. "I will stop by on my way in tomorrow and pick you up."

"What time?"

"I start around five am."

Regina was going to enjoy working with the energetic woman. As she dumped her tray and set it atop the shelf she had a moment of uneasiness. There were many things happening here that she wasn't aware of. Anger simmered at the idea she had been kept ignorant of the trials. She wondered what Laurel was doing, pushing for human trials so soon. The serum was safe, the delivery system also safe. But why the rush to get started?

She needed to get back to her quarters to check the project updates logged while she'd been in transit. It didn't sit well with her that the control was far from her. She was supposed to be a partner, not his latest lackey. She rubbed her stomach again. The bruises bothered her.

Regina's routine settled down in a couple weeks. She learned where the gym, labs and cafeteria were. She spent her days between her quarters and the labs, extending her hours worked to ten and sometimes twelve. The studies went the way she expected, except for the shortened timeline.

The weeks spent underground didn't bother her. She was too busy learning her way around and retesting her research, working with Dr. Laurel to integrate his cellular studies with her serum and helping to decrease the rejection rate. In some studies the injections into the epithelial lining were ineffective. They explored other avenues of delivery, finding those ways worked, though not as quickly as direct injection.

Every step forward brought its own rewards and failures. Using both animal and human results helped them fine-tune the delivery. The assistant Laurel brought with him was a mousy yes-man. His name was Yoseph Magellian, a man with no spine, yet a brain that seemed to work on every level all the time. She met him and then almost forgot he was there since he never seemed to leave the upper level where he lived with the mad scientist.

Dr. Laurel's research helped the serum to produce longer results than the twenty-four to forty-eight hour window for the strength she'd achieved before. Those animals injected with the updated form showed increased strength and aggression for seventy-two hours or more.

She didn't know too much about his part in the work. She understood he was using neurological-stimulators in small doses to regulate the test subjects use of the serum, creating a strength/aggression window five to ten times larger than any previous trials. The injections were into the stomach lining, the epithelial cells there were easier to reach and the organ accepted the serum with no side effects.

She recorded her data every day, spending time testing each batch of serum she and her assistants cooked up. She was determined to make sure her end of the trials was without errors.

Dr. Laurel, a demanding man, expected perfection in trials. Regina admired his mind, one of the greats in his field, yet she was not so fond of the man. His manner with the project, now she worked side by side with him, was cold and officious.

Old enough to be her father, he had the kind of voice in the labs that caused more than one of her assistants to cringe. Disciplined, he expected everyone around him to aspire to perfection. He wanted his reports emailed in specific fonts, his charts assembled a certain way, his coffee sweet and creamy. Regina was getting used to turning his rants aside and protecting her team with minutiae to distract him.

It worked, so far, and she was expert with the way he wanted things accomplished. She worked with her team, explaining to them the importance of following his instructions to the letter, as the reports they generated immediately went on to other scientists in the government. At least that's what she believed happened.

In only a few months the entire project functioned as a well-oiled machine, fewer rants from Dr. Laurel and better results in this second round of testing. They hadn't taken the final steps where the lighting would be used to trigger aggression in the men. She'd heard they were waiting for a commanding officer to oversee the training and development of the men into teams. Once they worked together, the final stage would begin.

Her days ended when she finished settling down the night watch. Keeping her lab secured was a priority. Even though no one would likely be nosy enough to go through her labs, she didn't want to grow complacent. This project wouldn't last forever. She'd be back in the scientific community as soon as she was done here.

When she finished checking her security, she usually headed for the cafeteria, thankful they operated like a regular base, on a 24/7 timetable. Grabbing a little something to eat, she wandered to her quarters to check emails. Most nights she changed clothes and headed to the huge gym facility. Working a round of weights then the pool for laps, she sometimes finished in the spa. If not, she walked back to her rooms for a shower and a midnight snack.

She smiled at familiar faces she passed in the halls, getting to know some of the military down here. One night early on, she ran into Coakley and Davidson in the gym.

"Hey, Doc." Coakley spoke as he spotted for Davidson.

"Coakley, Davidson, not much of a crowd." She dropped her towel and reset the weights. Taking her place, she worked beside the men.

"Nope, heard anything on the trials?" Davidson huffed a bit, sitting up when he finished his set. Once the first team were cleared for fieldwork, they were released for active trials under the influence. Transferred from the desert base, they moved to new quarters to train under the effects of the serum and the natural lighting provided by the sun and moon.

All reports were encouraging, but Laurel wanted to bring out more of the natural aggression in the men. That was in the second set of trials in the second team.

"Not yet. We have only heard good things from the previous team, so it's just a matter of time before you guys are called up." They'd heard that many times since Regina moved *Below*. It seemed her arrival both sped the timeline up and slowed it considerably for the others waiting.

It was true the reports were slower to come to her, usually through emails from Laurel. She kept the nickname to herself, afraid if she started using it it would slip out in front of him. The reports were glowing accomplishments, and she cheered every participant on. The current conversation brought her back.

"Hell, I'd take it for free," Coakley complained. "Getting real tired of waiting for nothing." He took Davidson's place, picking up the bar and beginning a set.

"I know it's difficult to wait, but hang in there." She huffed between lifts. She remembered her fantasy with them, had in fact used it a couple times to great results. Now she knew their personalities. They were like younger brothers, not so much fantasy fodder.

Both men actually smiled at her before retreating behind military masks. An officer had entered the gym. She wondered if he came standard issue, like the uniform. Finishing their workouts, the guys left. She studied the newcomer. He hadn't been there long. An email she received simply told her they were ready for the next step, since the officer for this base had finally arrived.

Chapter 4

She finished her short workout, waving at the guys as they left. Her thoughts moved back into the sexual arena. How could they not? The gym was far from deserted. Many of the soldiers wore nothing more than abbreviated shorts over hard bodies. So little was left to the imagination, at least hers, as they worked sets from machine to machine.

Regina left the gym as those thoughts began to awaken her libido. She tried not to catch the looks that followed her out. Too late, that stray thought crossing her mind brought her body screaming to life. Her nipples peaked against the t-shirt with her hyper awareness that they were watching her, fantasizing about her.

Really, though, she didn't think anyone would think twice about having a fling. She knew Tracy was regular with her soldier. She convinced the girl she should take a chance if her soldier was willing. If Regina had not seen them in the passage to her quarters, she would have noticed them somewhere else.

"I know he's the one for me," Tracy told her in the lab. Leaning over microscopes and jotting notes on the processes taking place left plenty of silence to fill.

While she cheered the lovers on, Regina knew their time here would end, and the soldiers' reassignments would take them all over the world. Tracy would go back to school to finish her education. Here, in this time out of time, they could believe it would last forever, letting the bond deepen and then seeing how far it would stretch once they were released from this project.

Her own needs were stretched thin. Even her continued work on other projects wasn't working as well as she'd hoped for a distraction. She tried to work into exhaustion, cutting off her growing libido with brain and bodywork. All she'd gotten was one hell of a taut body, toned and athletic. Her curves hadn't changed though, her breasts were still full, her hips still rounded. Yet a glance in a mirror showed bags and shadows under her eyes.

As she walked home her mind wandered through the months she'd been down here.

She'd heard somewhere the official military designation for this project was "Bio-shock". How very military to miss the definition of the project they funded. All had seemed to go well through the financing, and the military was solid behind the men who'd volunteered.

It was looking very successful and she was looking forward to starting the last trial, the last team. Everything was on hold for some unknown reason. It wasn't in her classification to know, and other than a stray question that floated through her mind, she didn't care. She was satisfied her work was sound and being proven every day, according to the waning emails. She figured the other trial teams were integrating well.

The only part of her days she didn't so much like happened to be the weekly injections of concentrated vitamins and minerals. Living underground put a strain on the body, which she understood. The injections kept her healthy, a needful condition. Her only objection was the needle. If she could drink the concoction, she would do so gladly.

The injection sight, her abdominal region, was the second issue. Of course it was a good place, not easily bumped or bruised and the flesh was fuller there and her arms and hips did not suffer. She endured them in silence. After all, all of the men on the trial teams took the injections without complaint. She still wanted to pout when she saw the bruises on her flesh.

It was only a matter of time before they would all be back under the sunshine, soaking up the real deal.

Every month she suffered injections to the side of her neck. Another concoction of vital nutrients Laurel insisted they needed. No one else mentioned them, so she didn't want to seem to be the only whiner for hating them. He chose times when she was alone in the labs to come to her with that syringe. It didn't contain much, but when he hit a nerve she cringed.

She hadn't made it out to shop in town in the months since she'd come *Below*. Somehow she'd been held back by questions from Laurel and missed the van out, or she'd been deep into another transcription and hadn't wanted the interruption. Her body relied on the injections because, while the food was great, her eating schedule was erratic.

The weekly staff meetings working with the military kept them to a semi-regular timeline. They covered all glitches, improvements, successes and failures. Open discussion and brainstorming practices offered solutions. It was where most of their information came together from topside, shared as needed. Regina attended them religiously, as hungry for the go-ahead as any of her team.

These meetings included the new commander, so he wasn't a stranger. He simply wasn't a talker. He focused on his job, his men. He was in charge of all military teams. These were his men, handpicked for this operation. She couldn't fault his choices. Every volunteer wanted to be here, wanted to participate eagerly in every facet of their trial. The last team she was especially close with, because they'd arrived here within days of each other.

Their commander had arrived a few months later. Mitch Bolton was a quiet man, rarely seen since his office and quarters were on the other side of the base from hers. He didn't spend time in her labs, and she appreciated one less demanding male peering over her shoulder, for now. That would soon change, so she couldn't help but wonder about the tall, dark male. He was no youth, closer to her age, past thirty years, surely. Command rested easily on his shoulders, his wide, strong shoulders. Like the rest of him, toned and tight, the muscles worked smoothly under the taut flesh that covered them. Opening her door, she leaned against it, thinking of the tall male.

"You need a cold shower." She dropped her workout clothes in a pile on the bathroom floor and stepped under the showerheads. The water drops caressed her flesh and did the opposite of cooling her off. Taking the handheld down, she rinsed the sweat and suds off. With one foot propped against the side of the tub she played the spray of water over her clit. She willed the faces of Coakley and Davidson before her closed eyes as pressure built using the familiar fantasy to reach relief. Her mouth watered to take one penis into her mouth and feel the other one slam against her clit. But as her climax built, the face that swam before her closed eyes morphed into Commander Mitch Bolton. She trembled as an orgasm climbed higher. Head back, she sobbed, when her body shook out of control. Leaning against the wall, she pulled calming breaths into her lungs.

Flipping the temperature knob to warm, she slipped to down into the shower, curling her legs under her.

"I need to get laid." She gave a wet smile, pushed her long hair out of her eyes. Still she couldn't banish the fantasy from her mind, his big body over hers, inside hers. Shaking the images off, she finished her shower.

This week's meeting opened like the others, discussion, issues, real coffee. The cafeteria kept everyone on decaf, so almost everyone *Below* existed on tea. No one favored decaffeinated coffee. As she took her seat she noticed more military uniforms were scattered around the room. After four months of human trials the first team was a success, as far as everyone reported, so the official nod to proceed arrived.

These must be the higher ups visiting. They never stayed long and never had an intelligent question for her. She dismissed them in favor of the announcement.

"Thank you all for being patient while those above compromised." Dr. Laurel stood behind the podium. "We began this testing with the first team of volunteers. The military volunteers were divided into three groups, as you know."

More notebooks were passed around with detailed groups assigned for the trials. Each thumbnail medical record accompanied a picture, biography and more stats and scores Regina did not recognize. None of the dossiers contained a legend to decipher them. She would study them at length later, when she had time to go over every detail. She gathered her load up and shoved them into her bag.

"Team one was released for real-time trials, an apparent success, with an acceptable loss of five percent in the first encounter." That was the first Regina had heard of losses. No reports of losses had come to her inbox. What else had she missed?

She did not feel like herself this morning. Could she be catching something? She'd gotten her latest injections two days ago. Maybe they threw her system off. The jump in her vitamin level with two injections so close together might have been too much. Maybe in the late night run to the cafeteria she'd gotten something less than fresh? Or maybe her body was craving real sunshine and the wind in her hair and a good fucking. She didn't know, but her lips curled in a smile. She bit them to banish the humor that ran through her mind while she listened to the rest of the discussion. She waited until the meeting adjourned to catch up with the mad scientist.

"Dr. Laurel, may I have a minute?" She hurried to his side. He'd left quickly with an officer in tow. She'd missed the high points of his speech. No matter, she'd get them later.

The officer with him stepped away. She'd seen him before, in the gym, in the cafeteria . . . in her midnight fantasies. Bolton, the new commander, she finally put it together in her head. Her mind worked slowly and she shook her head to clear it, force a focus she was far from feeling.

"Regina, what can I do for you?" Dr. Laurel turned to face her. His smile was false, impatient, and she guessed it was because of Bolton. She paused before speaking. Wondering where the impression that he wanted to avoid her came from, she covered her thoughts.

"I'm not feeling well. I wanted to let you know I am going home early. Is there anything I need to let my staff know before I leave?" He seemed to be studying her pale features and bloodshot eyes that had stared back at her from her mirror this morning. She almost took a step back at his intense scrutiny, unable to stop the recoil of her upper body. She tried to cover by shifting the stack of folders in her arm.

"Are you going to be okay?" He pinched her chin, holding her head back to catch more of the room's light on her face. "I wonder if you should keep the mineral injections in your stomach."

"No sir, the new site is fine." Her hand lifted to the back of her neck. The shots weren't the most pleasant there, but now her stomach was on a break from the daily routine. The bruises there were beginning to fade. She took a deep breath and focused on assuring Laurel again.

"I'll be fine. I think it's a little overwork and a midnight snack too late from the cafeteria. I wanted to rest and read over these." She tapped her full bag of dossiers. "Get to know a little more about our last set of test subjects before we start on them tomorrow."

"My dear, take the weekend. We all deserve some time to celebrate the successes so far. Let us plan on taking up the reins again on Monday." He dismissed her, but not before looking at her again. Satisfaction in his gaze when he released her chin made her shiver. Laurel looked over her shoulder to the officer. She guessed the man nodded but did not turn to look to see. It made Regina uneasy, but she shrugged it off, blaming it on her general shitty feeling.

She made her way back to her quarters. The door closed behind her with the soft whoosh she appreciated. Safe and secure behind that rock, she was guaranteed few interruptions. She used the communication unit in the kitchen to call the lab and let them know she was not coming back, passing along the things she knew Dr. Laurel would expect from them. She set the desk phone to privacy and headed to bed.

Refusing to catalogue how she felt, she stripped down to nothing, pulling the sheets up to her chin and struggled to sleep. Maybe if she rested her body everything would pass. Using meditation finally worked and she drifted into an uneasy slumber. Even as her body throbbed and burned under her skin, she felt as though she needed to shed it to become something else.

Moments ago Commander Mitch Bolton had stood in the shadows and watched the good doctor with his subordinate. The woman had looked pale, and that was saying something, for a woman who was naturally red haired. Her blue eyes looked gray in the florescent lights, and the circles under her eyes looked bruised. Her forehead glistened with a thin layer of clammy sweat. How could she have gotten sick? His information told him she never went topside. No exposure there, so whatever it was, she'd gotten it *Below*.

She was the one who had discovered the serum that had started this whole idea of the better soldier. Could she know she was setting them up? His whole command was about to be revved up artificially and sent out to kill. It was the worst-case scenario as far as he could see when the whole government needed to focus on how the hell to get all the soldiers back home.

Why make them better, stronger, more aggressive killers than they had to be? What if the serum, with the modifications through the hypothalamus, actually became permanent? What would the government do with these super killers? Realistically, they could not be at war forever. He slid his hands into his pockets, tamping down the fruitless anger he felt every time he thought of the project. It wasn't for him to decide. He followed orders. Disgusted, he watched the linguist as she left the room.

Dr. Laurel cleared his throat to get Bolton's attention. "I want the first of your last team in the lab tomorrow morning at 0600. We need to get some results to Virginia, let them know their dollars are paying off. I believe you are leading the last team in the final trial because you will be better able to gauge the improvements in your soldiers. I look forward to the next phase of our mission." He nodded and walked away, leaving Mitch staring after him.

When Laurel returned to join the General, Greg patiently waited for the good doctor to finish. He nodded at Mitch, falling in to step alongside the scientist.

Greg had said he wanted to speak with Mitch later, before leaving for home. Briefly Mitch wondered what he had to say, but he had a roster to set up and other things to accomplish. Whatever happened, not anything that went wrong could be placed at his feet. He turned to head to the office.

"Officious little prick."

"What was that, Commander?" Davidson walked up to him. He would be one of the first tested, starting tomorrow morning, no matter what the doctor told the linguist. Another wave of uneasiness skated across his mind. Laurel had outright lied to her. What game was he playing? What if she didn't know what was happening? She expected to start this testing in two days. If no one told her different, she wouldn't find out until it was a done deal, especially if she was sick.

He would have to rethink his opinion of her. This cast her in a different light altogether. Another innocent, much as Greg asked him to look for. Other than his soldiers, he hadn't really considered there would be an innocent involved.

Now look how the world had changed.

"Nothing, Kenny. Not important." Bolton shook off his unease. "Your team starts tomorrow on the serum." He started for his office with Kenny keeping him company.

"I can't wait, Commander. Wish we had a night or two topside, ya know. Have a few beers to blow off some of this steam, maybe find a girl . . ." He drifted off a little late. After all, this was his commander and he wasn't watching his words.

Mitch smiled. He knew perfectly well what Kenny was thinking. Mitch could see everything running in Kenny's mind. Of most interest to him was the erotic fantasy of the red haired doctor. The doctor was an obsession with him and his friend, Coakley. A stranger ménage he couldn't imagine.

"Where's Coakley? I thought you two were joined at the hip." Mitch paused at his office door. Kenny shrugged.

"He's busy. Our duty roster rotated and we're on separate shifts.

I'll get with him for dinner, unless he's made plans with Jackie. See ya later, Commander." He tossed a salute. Mitch nodded back, opening his door. He wanted to see who was in the first testing batch. He also wanted to explore why the good Dr. Laurel was starting tests without the linguist. He'd understood this to be a joint mission in R&D, so why the switch?

Another thing brushed his consciousness. Why was Dr. Laurel so interested in Regina Gardner Coombs' health? He hadn't missed the attention to every detail Laurel focused on his assistant.

He'd catalogued those details before. Opening his office, he moved inside, letting the door swing almost closed. He'd watched that lithe body cut through the pool, determination in every long stroke. She lifted free weights and used the machines when she wanted to run a circuit. That her body was curvy, had not escaped Mitch's notice. Her breasts were above average, her hips just right.

That red hair, so long underground without a cut, brushed her lower back when she left it down. The multicolored ends had faded to a uniform red as it grew out. In his fantasy that hair brushed his chest, her hot hands gripped his pectorals as she rose above him, helping maintain her balance as she rode him.

He snorted, pouring a nip from his smuggled bottle of bourbon. She never looked his way. He had a better chance of seeing her with Davidson and Coakley. He downed the smoky sip and went to work, shutting all thoughts of her from his mind and scolding his body into standing down. His cock had other ideas. Knowing he wouldn't concentrate with the lap full of need, he stepped into the adjoining bathroom and grabbed a paper towel. Imagining she knelt at his feet, he took his cock in hand and moved slowly, letting his pre-cum coat the engorged head. His balls grew heavy. His eyes closed as cum shot through his cock into his hand and the paper.

Chapter 5

The difference between the dossiers Regina received and the ones Mitch had was that he knew the meanings of the psi talent codes and she did not. He looked for commonalities between the groups and noted that physical talents and telekinesis, for one, made up the first group testing. Those exhibiting strong empathy, some with precognitive talents, made the second group.

It looked like the last group consisted of a mixed bag. With his inclusion, he figured the multi-talented subjects, including him, were leftovers. But maybe this group was the chosen successful group. There would be failures, no matter the results of the lab specimens. Some would die or be turned into vegetables. The only redeeming feature, as he remembered the general telling him, was that he had no letters to write to families. Every person *Below* was an only, with no living family and mid to high levels of psychic talents.

Not that it mattered, the current situation remained untenable. It was different on the battle lines, he fumed. One expected to die. It was something soldiers accepted or not. If a man made it every day and came home intact, congratulations, if he broke, the military took care of its own. Here, in the bowels of the earth, there was no war to fight. They were specimens for testing, simply animals kept in a larger cage.

He shoved the files into his desk, no need to lock them. Theft of information would have to come through the computer systems. No one could sneak down here and get out, not with the facility full of active duty military. It would be a war zone in no time. And a siege would never work here. Shaking his head at his troubled thoughts, he stretched in his chair.

Deciding to do a little investigating on his own, he headed to the labs. He had a few questions about the serum and the other injections everyone received. He hadn't been there often and wanted to see where Doc Reggie worked, needing to get a feel for the woman behind this farce, the one his men seemed to hold in high regard.

They'd been calling her Doc Reggie when he'd joined them, a title they used with a smile.

Down the corridors he stalked, a brooding presence keeping to the middle of the hallway where the light was dimmer. The fluorescents embedded in the ceilings at the top of the walls hummed and lit the walls. He moved quickly through the complex, his mind working on many levels. The more he tried to put together, the worse the picture became. He snorted. Leave it to pencil pushers to create a better warrior. In their grandiose scheme, they forgot the pawns they used to such advantage were human, something he could never forget.

He stopped at the hall junction, checking foot traffic by the lab. The lights were on, so the teams were still at it. No one walked the halls this late in the day. He hadn't realized he'd spent so much time reviewing the files again.

He turned the corner and entered the anteroom. Soon one of the research assistants came to see who was there.

"Hi, I wondered if I could ask you a few questions." Mitch didn't smile. His brooding smile would make the tech more nervous. He wanted straight answers and didn't have time to become a buddy. He had to be the equivalent of a bad cop, no good cop in sight.

"Um, sure. If you want to come in, follow me." The tech turned and led the way through a short hall with an office on either side and into the bigger room. Mitch could identify half of the equipment from high school chemistry and biology. The rest was beyond hazarding a guess.

"I need to watch this experiment a little closer, don't think I'm ignoring you." The Tech moved to a table with some of the equipment Mitch didn't recognize. Mitch watched him work several keyboards between three machines and then glance back to him, obviously waiting for his questions.

"Uh, hi. I'm Mike." He looked nervous having the commander pace the confines of the room. While the technicians were used to the neutral black uniforms, each man wore a patch on his shoulder denoting their branch of service. Naval dolphins embroidered in black decorated the man pacing around, Navy man.

"Commander Bolton."

Mike nodded.

No rank insignia showed, but Mitch knew the command in his manner would be difficult to miss. "This research." Waving a hand to encompass the whole of the lab, Mitch walked over to a clear area so he stood a better chance of not knocking something over. "Is it safe for us to be taking the serum?"

"Sure, it's totally herbal, all natural and as safe as smoking marijuana. The herbs don't stay to pollute the body. Because the natural ingredients of the formula simply hype the body for an extended time, the body metabolizes the herbs, flushing them out in waste." Mike swiveled on his stool to face Mitch from his hunched position. "In this instance, urine." He turned back to his study, face fused to a microscope. He turned to type information into the computer console.

"How does it work?"

"Well, Doc Reggie would be the one to ask for particulars. I know you military types don't do illegal, but, if you did smoke marijuana or know someone who did," He waited to see if the Commander acknowledged the question.

Dutifully, Mitch nodded.

"You know the effects, right? The smoker relaxes, his thinking seems confused and he thinks the ideas he has are genius. Smokers don't usually want to get aggressive, just passive. There's a lot of good thought behind making alcohol illegal and legalizing marijuana for that reason." Mike shook his head as though reminding himself to get back on course. After another flurry of clicks on the keyboard, he straightened his back.

"The high, if you want to call it that, wears off, leaving a serious case of the munchies, which you can prepare for ahead of time so you don't have these folks hopping into cars and driving. In time, the body takes the dregs of the herb and you piss them away. The body flushes itself and no harm done." He winked at the Commander, at ease with his subject.

"No harm done if done in moderation. I would not recommend living the high, which will cause some side effects. Nothing major, though. Herbs have been used for centuries, remember." Mike finished, glancing back at his experiment.

"And this mixture you want to inject into us?" Mitch led him along, crossing his arms, tensing to still the shiver that possessed him.

"Well, this mix is essentially the same. It's formulated from herbs that raise natural energy levels, like guarana and goto kola. These, mixed with a few other esoteric herbs Doc Reggie discovered and translated, will key an aggression, like too much adrenalin. Since it is natural, the heart is accepting the added load, proving the aggression and strength link. Once delivered by injection, the herbs incite the reaction in the body. The subject will stay in the aggressive/strength mode until he recognizes safety. When the high wears off, the subject seems to experience a letdown."

"Side effects?" Mitch leaned his hip against a slate topped table.

"Few to none. As I said, the most we have experienced is with some of the longest overdosed specimens. They seem to crash hard when kept juiced in perceived 'enemy territory'." Mike used air quotes with his fingers, finally taking them from the keyboard.

"There have been two fatalities in three years of animal testing. One we discovered had an aneurism in the brain, which blew out and flooded the brain. The other one, same thing, that aneurism hit the heart. Neither one of them actually related to the formula, but resulting from the increased strain on the system."

"From what Dr. Laurel told us this afternoon, we start testing tomorrow morning. How many batches of the serum are ready for humans?"

"Tomorrow? Doc Reggie called to let us know we get the weekend off. We weren't supposed to start until Monday." Mike's voice rose into a whine and then he sighed. "Damn military, their annoying quirk of wanting it yesterday." Mike collected himself with a glance back at his screen and a quick run over the keyboard. He turned to look back at the commander, absently scratching his head.

"Well, we have enough to get everyone in this facility for the next two years, as long as we inject on a month-by-month basis. With Dr. Laurel's work on the epithelial cells, cells which surround every organ in the body and the hypothalamus region of the brain, it lasts longer than a quick boost," Mike explained, doing a bit of math in his head.

Mitch froze. He hadn't expected that. The sheer amount of serum housed here boggled his mind. What if they were planning to inject large numbers of GIs with this? It hadn't taken them long to manufacture an appalling amount of the drug. He needed to talk with Greg more than ever.

His head spun with the information the tech had unloaded, for now he couldn't think of any more questions. Rather, this tech could not answer the questions he had to ask. He needed a research linguist with biological training. Luckily, he knew where she lived.

He thanked the tech, told him he'd see him in the morning and escaped. Mind whirling with more and more questions, he paused in the corridor. Go to her now or leave it for later? He rubbed his head, hoping to stave off a headache.

Maybe he should eat, leave the questions until later, when he had a plan of attack. He turned toward the cafeteria. Mitch winced as he rubbed a hand across his chest. Those injection sites bothered him more now that he understood what was being done to his body. He was slightly comforted to know about the side effects, but only slightly. He sighed and entered the cafeteria. He'd watch, for now, take action when needed.

General Greg Dolca washed his hands, rinsed and washed them a second time. Exposure to Laurel always left him feeling slimy. He'd talked with the man he'd heard referred to as the mad scientist. The program wasn't working the way Laurel had assured them it would.

Real world testing had been a bust. That news hadn't filtered down here, since they were trying to keep a tight lid on it all. He needed to speak with Mitch before he left, touching base to make sure he was doing okay here, that the serum hadn't caused any abnormalities yet. The tests finished above ground were royal fuck-ups. Just how bad even he wasn't sure.

However, instead of giving up on the project, Dr. Laurel had convinced the higher ups that those tests differed from the testing about to begin *Below.*

When the higher ups had insisted on using Mitch for this assignment, Greg had balked. All his protests had been brushed aside. Like Mitch, he followed orders. Still he needed to talk to his cousin.

It was now a matter of time for Mitch, and Greg was sick with worry. He'd called his mother, asking for any information that might help Mitch, without giving her any idea it was for her nephew. She assured him all was well. The basics were covered as he'd grown. There was a slight hesitation, and he picked up on the hitch.

What she told him next had him sitting down quickly and grabbing his desk to keep upright. The DNA was selective, meaning that it would choose to expose some of the family to another form, twisting bones and growing skin that was far from human. It was what gave breath to the legends of werewolves and such.

He'd tried to laugh it off, but she'd spoken of family who'd been afflicted with that form of it. It seemed to have skipped his siblings. She admitted to him she'd changed forms on occasion when stresses were too much and her body chemistry was off balance. Sick to his stomach, he hesitated to ask about his uncle. He'd let the information sink in.

And after that he'd asked about Mitch.

He made it his priority to see Mitch before he left, but his cousin couldn't be found and the car was waiting topside for him. He could get in touch with Mitch through emails, but that was less than optimal for the news he had to break to him about his biological make up. Greg also wanted to tell him about the failure rate, one hundred percent fatalities in the first two teams to be released. Mitch was right, this was a huge mistake. It had taken on a life of its own, and Greg could not stop it.

Cursing fate that kept them apart for now, he took his place in the helicopter and buckled up. When the bird lifted he stared at the little house hiding in the desert. He prayed these new trials would unlock the secret of control. He didn't like the nightmares that formed as he thought   of   Mitch   and   the   uncertain   DNA.

Chapter 6

The work on the trials proceeded smoothly. Several groups were treated, tested, and transferred out to integrate with standard military precision. Beyond the first injections, Regina made sure Laurel knew her displeasure with the changed timeline, excluding her for the first two days.

She'd had a rough weekend, trying to throw off whatever bug ate at her. She'd been chilled and burning by turns, suffered with body aches like the flu, yet she had no other signs of being infected with the bug. She'd eaten some soup Tracy brought her and sipped herbal tea until she floated. Tracy stayed with her and slept on the couch when she'd heard Regina was sick, leaving her lover alone all weekend.

The woman never had a quiet moment, so Regina listened until she dozed off, hearing the tone follow her into slumber. By the next day she was stronger and so angry with Laurel she got up to call him and tell him what she thought of his lying to her. Tracy convinced her otherwise and she relented. The conversation she was going to have with him still played in her head.

Feeling better, she caught up to the trials in no time, once Monday rolled around. She'd gotten some rest and felt a little better. Fatigue dogged her every footstep, but she was getting used to that shadow hanging around.

She turned over the soldiers to Dr. Laurel and Commander Bolton after making sure the serum worked properly and the feedback she received assured her there were no lasting issues. She knew this form of testing was top secret in lower levels than she had clearance to go.

Team coding those test subjects into A1, A2 and A3, she did receive emails on the results of the serum, lighting and the extended lifetime of the trials in actual practice.

She was pleased this worked, that the men did not suffer side effects. When testing and training finished for the day, down time was simply that, they came back to safety and relaxed. Most of them slept away the remains of the formulation and woke up refreshed and ready to go again. All serum levels dropped close to zero in blood samples taken from each of them before breakfast. Everything worked as it should, allowing her to relax.

The one thing she stressed over personally was the mental over-stimulation. It worried her that feeding off the aggression might permanently change the personality of a subject. Rats and men were a universe apart in the brain department. While strong, aggressive men were perfect fantasy material for the bedroom, or fantastical material for a new army, it would not do to have that turned on women or other men with malicious intent. The stretch from soldier, to bully to complete psychopath was not so far.

Regina finally understood the psi scores, having decisively cornered Dr. Laurel and asked him to explain. It made a kind of sense to her. If the brain were already using more of the sheer available computing power, the effect of the serum was lessened by the strength of the mental discipline already in use.

A real side-effect she noticed in some of the men was a growing incidence of the cluster headaches usually brought on by seasonal changes. The underground facility had no seasons. It is not a common type of headache. About two people in 10,000 had them. These headaches mostly affected men, but Regina was finding she had begun to experience them as well.

Current theory attributed them to the biological clock of the brain or the hypothalamus. No biochemical evidence pointed to the actual cause. Maybe they occurred in the case of these men because they lived under the artificial lighting.

She sent emails out to see if the incidents increased or lessened in the men integrated into life topside. No mention showed that the headaches ever returned. She had to figure it was underground living.

She made note of it in her journal and reported it to Dr. Laurel. He actually came to her lab to speak with her about the headaches. She didn't have any further knowledge and told him so. He watched her with those mad scientist eyes and finally patted her on the arm like a child before leaving her.

It was becoming regular, everyone referring to Dr. Laurel as the mad scientist. He seemed to be way too close to the subjects of this trial, taking daily checks with all of the participants. He was also in her lab several times a day, putting her staff off balance with his driving questions. While Regina knew how important this was to the government and the military, she kept herself removed from the test subjects for her objectivity and her piece of mind. She kept Laurel's interruptions to a minimum to protect the sanity of her staff, while using other tactics to pull him away from the actual work.

Her days were full and her nights cold and lonely. Yet there was one man she tried to block from her mind. He'd taken root there and was in no rush to hurry out. She had allowed him to weave his way into her fantasies, guiding her through orgasms many nights when she fell into bed exhausted, yet too keyed to sleep. Perhaps that explained why he wasn't leaving. He was a big man, dark featured, powerful, brooding and handsome as sin. She worked with him daily now as he conducted the physical training with his men.

He followed his team's duration, aggression and strength while under the influence as closely as any scientist *Below.* His turn was coming up for the last treatments and she could imagine that hard body beneath her hands. He shattered her objectivity every time he appeared. Shaking her to the core with every appearance, he never took obvious notice of her, simply strode into the lab and commandeered her workstation.

Though he could use any other monitor on the floor, he moved into her personal space every day. A dark tease, a temptation she could barely resist, he blew her concentration every time he moved through the doorway.

Bolton recorded the sessions with his men, using her terminal in the lab. Sometimes he was still sweaty from the gym when he showed up to make his notes. He recorded them in her office because it was closest to the actual working trial space, or so he'd told her once when she'd managed to ask. He stopped by often and sent his information by email to his office, then he worked from there to collate everything he noticed.

He'd become a specter in her work day, interacting with her lab much like Laurel. He never made anyone anxious, if she left herself out of the equation. They'd gotten to first name basis, replacing the unwieldy Commander Bolton with the now familiar Mitch. He called her Doc Regina most of the time, following the nickname she'd been given by his men. Yet there was a rare "Regina" mixed in. She found herself smiling around him, watching his every movement, hypnotized at his arrival. It wasn't until he left the lab that she wondered how much of an idiot she appeared to him and her staff, mooning over the big man.

She noticed him every time, inhaled his scent and stored him in her memory. There was more to him. Invested in his position, strong without being overbearing, he was a no nonsense officer. She wanted that fierce control for herself. She was coming to need the obvious strength of him she feared she would never find.

Commander Mitch Bolton wore the mantle of authority as if he was born to rule. It appealed to her in some primitive place deep within her psyche. She was a sunflower, turning to follow him, needing him to feed something deep inside. She hid the feelings, clenching her teeth and every muscle as he moved in and out of her presence, fighting not to give away any hints of what he was doing to her.

Today he joined them, still breathing hard from the gym. His shorts didn't hide the shape and size of his cock and balls. He stalked into her lab and went straight to the office, taking her computer and chair. A supreme male animal, he reminded her of a lion with his hair mussed and wild about his head.

A flurry of keystrokes and almost fifteen minutes later he left, again without a word. He glanced her way and nodded. The door whispered shut behind him. He left the scent of unique male musk of man and sweat filling her office. She kept the door closed to trap the scent trace of him in the air. Each deep breath stirred hard cramps low inside her body. She ached to belong to him, to be claimed by his strength, his power. Hunger clawed at her long after he was gone and she slipped into daydreams of being with him, a sweaty coil of bodies.

She tried to work after he left, but the discomfort derailed every thought.

Mitch's heart pounded. He couldn't get her out of his head today. She was close and so far from his reach. He had no business getting close to her and the little ruse he'd used to get close to her, sharing her personal space, was whirling out of control. He needed to see her daily, needed to be close to her. A kid in a candy store he wasn't, yet he was kept away from her by convention. He was an officer in a biological trial, he was responsible for his men and their wellbeing, he didn't need to be lusting after a woman he couldn't have, couldn't keep once this project finished.

She was the doctor in control of the serum they injected daily now, their time under the lights not far away. His men were well trained. He'd worked them hard and the payoff should help control the rage the serum would unleash. Every time he got close to her, his body fought his command, wanting contact. Wanting far more than contact, hell, he wanted her naked and panting under him.

He'd closed his eyes, knowing she watched him from outside her small office. He'd moved straight here, trying to keep his distance but needing his fix. She'd been talking with Mike and Tracy and he'd barely nodded hello.

There, her singular fragrance filled the air, lending him something he needed to survive. That was a dangerous sign and he'd fought it until he'd lost. Now all he could do was be close to her, see her and watch over her. His suspicions were coming home to be counted and he hadn't missed his guess on any so far.

Need roared inside of him, a hungry beast demanding what he should never have.

It wasn't as if he noticed her, Regina thought as he left her office. Other than the curt nods of his coming and going, he'd rarely spoken to her. He'd begun to spend time near her after her weekend illness. She glimpsed him frequently around her. For months they'd been together, yet he'd stayed away, hidden on his side of the base. All she'd had were dreams spun out of nothing solid, but real to her. Now he was close, yet they were no closer personally and the daily torture gathered, wearing on her with the hunger he incited.

Oblivious to time passing, Regina leaned back in her chair, soaking in the musky scent of him fresh around her. Another deep breath and she closed her eyes. She'd been so busy with the studies, she'd forgotten it was the anniversary of her divorce. She and her husband had left their marriage long before their signatures hit the bottom line.

Was that why she hungered for Mitch, a male in his prime, unlike most of the kids in the program? Sitting back, all she could think about was wrapping her body around Mitch Bolton.

For two dry years she had had to ease every itch by herself when one surfaced. She realized she'd simply slipped back into the routine she kept during her marriage. Her needs sublimated into her work.

Playtime did not exist.

Now, before Mitch would join the trials, his every move recorded, she could reach out for him. Maybe he was surfing his own dry spell. Suddenly she devoutly hoped so. There had to be a way. She needed a plan and a time they could reach out to each other.

Unable to find a cause for the cluster headaches, sleepless nights and the general malaise that lingered, she blamed it on lack of consensual sex. She'd weathered the flu or whatever brought her down not long ago, but the reason for it escaped her.

Maybe she should have searched for someone and simply gotten laid. There were many males *Below*, but none attracted her more than the commander. She seriously had a crush on him, unable to label it anything else. Regina laughed at her musings. She needed to screw her courage up to ask him to dinner.

Against the orders weekly delivered by the mad scientist, she was ready to join the informal mutiny on that particular front. She wanted to mingle with a test subject, this specific one. She was tired of doing without when she suspected everyone else was having sex.

Hells bells, Tracy and her guy were working out long-range plans. God's balls, even Mike was spending time with someone special, very special in a don't ask, don't tell situation that encompassed the entire population *Below*.

There would be no working this afternoon, not after Mitch's stormy arrival and hasty exit. She closed her journal, exited the workstation and left a few instructions behind. Regina locked her office and headed back to her quarters. Inside her apartment she kicked off her shoes and opened the bedroom closet.

Her clothes were a dismal array of business attire, lab scrubs and her exercise togs. She wondered how she could catch his attention in those. Shaking her head, Regina smiled. It wasn't as if she could plan a date. As soon as she took goods from the cafeteria to cook in her place the whole neighborhood would know. There could be no secrets down here.

On the plus side, her body was in the best shape of her life. The time *Below* had to be spent someway, and the gym was state of the art with every kind of machine manufactured. When something new came out the military wanted one or two and they shipped it in and installed it. If he could jumpstart her libido in workout clothes, maybe she could return the favor.

All she had to do is make sure they happened to be in the gym or the pool at the same time. He might be headed for the pool right now, or one of the spas. It was a simple matter to change and head that way. She rushed toward the chest, not wanting to waste a single second now she'd made her decision.

The light on her laptop warned her of new email. She wanted to walk past it, ignoring the flash insisting she take note. She did walk past it, feeling guilty as she pulled on her swimsuit. Still arguing the pros and cons, she stopped on her way out and woke the machine up to get the message.

After all, it could be from Laurel.

Hey girl,

Hope life is being good to you. Since I can't reach you any other way, I sent you this   email. This caught my eye and I wanted to see if these were some of those "Regina's Rangers"   you   left   to work on. It's not the best news.

Anyway, was thinkin' of you and missing you.

I'm marrying Donald in the spring. He's the right one for me. You know you're invited,   but I doubt you'll come. Talk to you later, Reg. Take care.

Regina opened the attachment, managing to send off a lighthearted if impatient answer while the attachment was dutifully scanned for viruses. She watched the six minute clip.

She watched the video clip again, wondering if Mitch knew about this. The report was jumpy, since the video feed was unsteady, likely taken by a phone and an individual who wanted to remain anonymous, but that did not change the story. Regina picked up the phone and called to see if she could get a number for the commander through the switchboard. Luckily, the operator connected her to his room. No swimming today, she thought when his voice growled in her ear.

"Bolton."

"Mitch, it is Regina. Do you know where I live?"

"Yeah, what's up?" She imagined him dripping from his shower, swiping at runnels of water one handed.

"I have something you need to look at." She set the receiver back in the cradle without giving him time to respond. He would be here shortly. She glanced around the spotless room, wondering if anything needed straightening, her mind shying away from the email.

Before he arrived, she downloaded the email to a file she then secured under a password. Then she sent it to a third party secure storage facility. Deleting the email, she went to the door when she heard the chime. He was here.

"Come in."

When he looked at her from head to toe she remembered she was still dressed to go swimming. "Don't ask."

"What have you got?" he asked her as the door closed behind him. He glanced around the room, needing to pry his gaze off her. He was glad he'd worn loose pants and kept his shirttail out, keeping his body well hidden in its sudden reaction to Regina, the woman. *My woman*, something primal growled in his mind.

The cold shower he'd taken lost its effect the second she opened the door. He struggled to focus on what she was saying instead of what she was barely wearing. He'd seen the suit before from a distance in the gym. Up close, the expanse of creamy flesh begged for a nibble and lick. Hell, he wanted to bite and leave his mark for all to see. Forcing his mind to what she was saying, he cleared his throat and nodded.

"I received an email from a friend. She thought this was a joke, but these are my guys." She turned the laptop to face his way and started the video. *"Our* guys." Looking anywhere but there, she studied him as he watched the news clip. His dark hair, always a little long, was starting to curl around his neckline. She'd guessed right about the shower. His hair was still wet and clumped and smelled like shampoo. She wanted to brush that luxurious hair back when it fell over his eyes. He raked his fingers through it with one hand and reached to restart the clip with the other hand. Like Regina, he watched the video loop a couple of times. After the first expression of shock, his face was shuttered and unreadable. His eyes focused on the reporter, he sank to her chair.

"This can't be."

"Okay, I believe you." Regina leaned against the bar, not five feet away. Her arms crossed over her flat stomach pushing her breasts up.

"No, what I mean is—"

"Yeah, I know what you mean. Twenty men, the first two groups

50

released, have been wiped out—"

"By friendly fire."

She wanted to use air quotes for his words, but her arms were helping to keep her strong, holding in the harsh emotions tearing at her. "Why would our own military kill those teams?" Regina crossed the room and curled up on her sofa. She tucked her bare feet under her, coiling into a ball of pain. "Is it our fault?" She breathed the question, unable to accept.

"No, by all the gods, it's not our fault. I need to get some messages sent. There has to be an explanation for this. All the testing is safe, it works and there are no side effects. The guys all come down and are fine, repeatedly. How would killing them benefit?" He started pacing as he thought.

Chapter 7

Her mind still pulling up picture after picture, Regina watched him stalk around her living room. Davidson was in the first group and Coakley in the second. She remembered them both, Coakley whispering naughty things to her while under her care, Kenny Davidson such a clown. The two men she could have played with when she first arrived underground.

Others stood out, Simpson and his friend Simonson, together since boot, one a six foot six giant and the other four eleven. Mason, Glade, Russell, the list of names went through her mind, matching personalities to faces. All of them dead, caught in a deadly crossfire, killed by their brothers in arms.

Regina didn't realize she was crying until Mitch handed her a paper towel. She looked up at him, puzzled.

"You sniffled." He settled into the cushions beside her as she blew her nose. The anger he'd worn like a cloak had tempered. He simply pushed it aside for now as he struggled to reason with what he'd watched.

"Sorry," she croaked, "I see them all, every smile, hear every curse."

"I know. I sent out a couple of feelers, using secured lines and encryptions. I don't know if I can find out anything, but I'll give it a shot." He turned to face her. "I guess I don't have to tell you no one can know this." When she turned to him he felt like he'd kicked her. She looked wounded, diminished somehow. He wanted to reach out to her, hold her, his body moved to do that, give her comfort. He stopped by sheer force of will. Now was not the time to give in to these feelings. Would that time would ever be?

"I don't even know—" She started speaking, her voice broken, shaking her head. She glanced back to the laptop when the light started blinking. Another email arrived.

"I should check that." Regina untangled her legs and opened the mailbox. She couldn't believe her eyes.

"Mitch, you won't believe—" Then he was standing behind her. His breath gusted hot on her bare shoulder as he read the email.

It was the latest update on the teams in the field and around the world. All soldiers were active and alert. No side effects, including the headaches she recorded in the lab, reported by any team members. Orders existed for the next team as soon as their release from routine testing.

"Son of a bitch," Mitch growled. "Who sent this fucker?" His eyes tracked back up the listing of stats linked to soldiers, finding the last address. Dr. Emerson Laurel forwarded this to her. The sender's address was encrypted and coded, but Mitch recognized it as a local one.

"These are false emails. They are being generated and sent from here, but why?" He raked a hand through his drying hair. Regina forwarded them as usual, filing hers in the folder in case she would ever need them again.

She turned as Mitch stalked away from her to resume his pacing. What other lies had they been told? Her left eye started watering and she knew to prepare for another headache. She hoped this cluster would fade quickly, even though she knew it would return in a while.

The pain hit her eye like a freight train, full steam. She dug the heel of her hand into her eye socket, pressing against the sudden agony. Her heartbeat throbbed through her hair follicles, she knew for a fact hair could hurt. As a doctor, she knew her eyeball would not pop out, but the thought of the relief that would bring made her wish. She sighed and stood up slowly, joining Mitch in wearing a walkway in her living room.

"What's wrong?" He stared at the hand holding the side of her head.

"Another headache, you know the ones. Like your eye is going to explode, your hair hurts, you have to move or die." She looked up at him, her eye streaming. She found some tissue and wiped the tears.

"Why are you getting them?" He watched her as dreadful pieces fell into place. Suspicions he'd hoped were wrong now seemed probable. His most recent deduction, given all the information and the scheduling of injections, was based on her. The mad scientist had prepped Regina for the serum as well as him and his men. He would bet his last paycheck that she did not have a clue.

"Are you taking the injections?" he asked when she stopped to turn in her row of pacing.

"No, not the trial. We haven't introduced it to women yet. I'm taking the vitamin/mineral cocktail to keep up to operating in a sunless environment, like everyone else." Distracted, she rubbed her temple, shaking her head.

"You haven't been out to town since you got here?" Mitch's stomach clenched. He studied her body as she walked around his own path. There, beside her navel, a small bruise darkened her taut flesh. That was the proof he needed. Walking up behind her, he wrapped his hands around the muscles tight at the nape of her neck. He felt uncomfortable invading her mind, but he needed answers and need them now. He couldn't protect her if he didn't know exactly her role in this fiasco. Carefully he probed her thoughts. He'd always been able to do this, something his mother shared with him, but his father refused to acknowledge. There were other things in his family that hadn't been discussed.

He'd fallen from a tree, landing on his elbow. Sure that his arm was broken, he'd headed in to tell his parents. By the time his father took his arm and rotated it the pain and redness were fading. He'd never gotten sick, even a cold, while his play and school mates were stricken time and again with childhood maladies.

This mind-speak, his mother had cautioned him to never say anything to his father. He'd wondered about it when he was older, then simply kept it to himself. His mother had cautioned him that it was invasive and rude when he was younger. As an adult, he'd used the talent judiciously, not for his sake but to find the root of issues that he had strong misgivings about.

She moaned and dropped her head forward. Taking a hand from her face, she collected her hair and pulled it over her shoulder. It had gotten longer down here. She sighed as Mitch spread his fingers, looking to relax those muscles. She didn't know he was checking her flesh to see if she carried bruises there.

"No, Tracy was always headed out, so she would pick up things I needed or wanted. I'm a slave to the work." Regina stiffened then relented. His hands were hot and that heat loosened tense nerves. As he rubbed and prodded the stiffness out, she sighed. This time the headache passed in a few minutes. As always, she ached after they passed, feeling bruised in her eye socket and her brain. His hands eased, lightly stroking her. The rubbing becoming a caress.

Regina sighed with relief at his touch. "Thank you, that's much better."

He didn't answer. He found a cluster of spots, the same place as his injection site, the same area all the men had been injected. Vitamins and minerals? Laurel lied to her, just as he lied to them in his email. Disgusted with his confirmed theory, he lowered his hands from her, clenching them into fists to capture and hold the softness of her skin to his palms. Regina had no idea of the extent of Laurel's duplicity.

The mad scientist was taking a chance by using his colleague as a test subject. What was the real experiment here? Deciding to keep his council for the time being, he would stay closer to Regina Gardner to find his answers. It was only a matter of time now that he'd blown the whistle. The last email went to his cousin, the general. He'd attached every bit of evidence he'd acquired. It was time to pull the plug on this fatal experiment.

She might be the only woman in the trials. Who knew what could happen to her when she was exposed to the light therapy that accompanied the injections? There was no need to burden her or make her fearful. Protective instincts rose, clenching his body and making him ache that he couldn't keep her free of the problems he suspected hovered on the near horizon. She'd had a crushing blow today. He shook his head. Twenty men lost, and the last team of ten, his best-handpicked team, waited for the trials.

Regina shuddered as his thumbs stroked across the back of her neck. His touch set flame to her body, as she'd known it would. If she backed against him, would his body be as aroused as hers? His breathing quickened when he stood behind her, rubbing out the stiffness in her neck and shoulders. She needed someone to hold her, with the twenty deaths so close to her. She turned to face him, snaked her arms around his waist and she pulled herself close to his body.

Mitch stiffened, and then gave in with a sigh. His arms wrapped around her, tucking her under his chin and along his body. His erection thrust against her stomach and he wondered if she would pull away. His answer came as she undulated against him in a sensuous, snakelike movement.

The timing sucked, and he wanted answers, *needed* them to make some kind of sense. His men were dead for no discernible reason. Regina was marked for the serum like everyone else here, with no consent on her part that he understood. He needed to gather background intelligence on the mad scientist. His suspicion fell firmly on Dr. Laurel, yet he wondered how far up the chain this disaster climbed.

He had no way to call HQ and speak with the general. With testing beginning in hours, he wouldn't be allowed topside until this phase was over. Yet his gut assured him once this trial ended, so would the experiment. Worried about the body count, he wanted to hunt down the mad scientist and beat the truth out of him.

Regina's needs eclipsed that impulse.

The feel of her in his arms called to everything male inside of him, derailing his train of thought. She was the unknown and the unattainable. She was untouchable, a doctor focused on her experiment, which happened to be Mitch. No one, other than a saint in such close quarters *Below*, ever got close to her. He'd listened to the rumors about her. Not that anyone labeled her an ice queen. She was dedicated and cared about each of the people she met. There was an air about her that simply told one to look but don't touch, as though getting down and dirty was beyond her.

If she kept that needy squirming against him, things were going to get down between them right now. Her nails scored his back, drawing a moan up his throat. He pulled her away from his body, fighting her hold, fighting the need rising inside him. Another animal moved within his skin, one that had no doubts it wanted everything she wanted to give.

Her gaze snapped up to him, stormy and questioning. Her hips rocked pressing against his cock. He was aware only nylon separated her from him. He could move his hands lower and slide his palms along that fine ass and cup her to him.

Regina moaned, needing this for so many reasons. The longer she stayed in contact with him, the rest of the reasons slipped away, leaving the only one that mattered. He was male and she was female. It was the original primal equation. She watched the conflict cross his features, his breathing labored. She bet he didn't know he was pumping his hips in the give and take dance led by hers. This was wrong in so many ways. He was an officer under orders to submit to the experiment, she was the doctor hired to test him. Her body ignored her mind.

Regina wanted to feel his skin burn against hers. She was tired of waiting. Now the genie was out of his two-year bottle, she wanted to feel again. She bunched the material of his shirt in her hands, pulling it up so she could slip her hand across his broad back. His lids drifted to half-mast, shadows obscured his pupils but she knew they were as blown as hers were. She didn't need a biology degree to know that, his cock, throbbing in time with her heartbeat, pressing insistently against her stomach proved it. She pressed into him again, his hands finally easing the grip that held her away.

Mitch reached over his shoulder and grabbed a handful of shirt, pulled it over his head and tossed it to the floor. Her breasts, nearly coming out of her suit, plumped against his skin. Her nipples, hard erect points, dug into his chest. Her hands dipped into the small of his back. One of them explored below his belt. Her fingertips tickling the rise of his ass. He bucked against her body, tangling his fingers in her mussed red mane, pulling her mouth to his. He took her mouth as he would take her body, deep and hard. When her taste flooded him, he gentled the kiss, leading her. She tasted of tears and need, a softly feminine flavor he wanted more of, so he took it.

Regina followed his lead with deft precision he'd never noticed. She unfastened his slacks and let them slide down his long legs. She smiled against his lips. He pulled back, finally catching a breath before her hand swept around his cock. She watched him as her hand explored his length and thickness. His features tightened in a pained grimace as her fingertips learned his heat, followed the ridge of the crown around to the surgical indent where a drop of fluid eased from his body.

Her other hand cupped the furry sac containing his balls. She rolled them in her palm, tugging on them. Mitch's head dropped back. A moan rose up from his chest. His hands tightened on her shoulders. She would have bruises later, and she was okay with every one. His big body shuddered when she wrapped both palms around his shaft, stroking the length of him and back to the base.

Mitch jackknifed and swept her into his arms, dislodging her hold. He paused to toe his shoes off and kick his pants away. Into the bedroom he carried her to drop her onto the bed. He stalked up her body, intent on getting her naked as he was. He pulled one bikini tie loose from her hips and swept the bit of fabric away from her hipbones, smiling as her red cap came into view. That same hand plundered her slit, stroking through her swollen labia to the goodies hidden within. Watching her with feral eyes, he brought his hand to his lips, licking her flavor from every finger.

Regina froze. The look in his eyes and the carnality of his actions immobilized her for the moment. He exuded raw sex and power. She eased back onto the covers. One hand pulled the other string at her hip and the other moved to the tie behind her head. She lifted her hips and Mitch tugged the bottoms away and tossed them off the bed. He reached up to her other hand, stopping the tug that would release her breasts from the bright fabric of her suit. His body slipped between her spread thighs, his hips brushing the throbbing length of his cock along her heat. She writhed against him, her hips rising to meet his.

Mitch pulled both strings down to her collarbones, riding her shudder as the strings pooled on her skin. He loved how responsive her body was, shivering under his. He dropped his head to recapture her lips. She met him half way, her hunger growing. Her impatient nipping at his lips pleased him into smiling. His hunger raging to be free, he fought to ignore the primal force roaring through his body. He wanted this to last. He'd earned the freedom to touch the untouchable after eight interminable months. He wanted every memory etched unforgettably in his head, on his body.

He moved his mouth to her jaw, to her ear. Always caressing her with his lips and tongue, even biting her, loving her wanton reaction to his violence, he never lost contact with her body. He shifted his weight, his arms braced beside her arms, holding them next to her ribs. Taking a string in his mouth, he peeled the cup away from the breast beneath. Regina arched up to him in supplication. He ignored her moans, tight little sounds broadcasting her growing need. The second strap followed the first. As the cup pulled away leaving her exposed to his gaze, he lowered his head and captured her taut nipple between his lips.

Her nipples rose in the freedom, spearing upward on the luscious peaks. Peach and coral, they looked delicious. He kissed them, licking them and driving her wild between his arms.

"You taste so good." His heavy growl of a voice vibrated against her skin, the words pulled from somewhere deep.

Her arms fought free of her sides. She tangled her hands in his hair, pulling him down to her, urging him to her body with forceful tugs. He resisted her, instead nipping and licking the distended fleshy points with bare contact. The beautiful shades of her body reminded him of peaches and cream. The tips of her breasts darkened with his ministrations.

Unable to resist any longer, he opened wide and took as much of her into his mouth as he could. He sucked her flesh, leaving ridges in her creamy skin with his teeth, the first marks claiming her as his. He pulled off her slowly, letting his teeth and tongue press her nipple to the roof of his mouth, tugging the firm flesh. With a slurp, he let one go and engulfed the other, treating it the way he did first.

"Mitch." Her breathy moan rose to a near scream as heat bloomed from his mouth through her. The touch echoed to every nerve ending, sensitizing her entire body. Waves crashed through her womb. The muscles of her pussy grasped at nothing. Her body writhed beneath his and he settled his body to hers to keep her knees away from sensitive parts in her sensual dance. She grasped his sides, hands roving his back, nails biting as she struggled to find a center point in a chaotic universe of pleasure she'd never before experienced. He'd barely touched her and she was a wet mess.

He knew women enough to realize his touch, his kisses to her flesh, were bringing her to orgasm. The breathless pants and groans, the shudders and arching against him told him the story. He pushed her over the first precipice, enjoying her release with her. When she eased he stiffened his arms, rising above her to look at his marks on her breasts.

Her hands fell away from his hair, taking in gulping breaths as her body slowly recovered. He backed his hips off her body, pulling away from her heat, the kiss of wetness along the underside of his cock making him hunger for a taste.

Between her legs, he draped her thighs over his shoulders. He parted the swollen folds, the fiery curls now dotted with her cream, glistening honey she spread over his cock. He licked the path his hand took earlier, touching her with a fleeting stab. Regina bowed to his mouth, her breath whooshing out of her. He smiled against her slick flesh at the sound. He hunched his shoulders closer to her, lowering his head and taking control of her again.

Chapter 8

Regina barely recovered her mind from the first round of sensations before he started again. His superior size and strength kept her locked into place. He was dominant, unexpected and exciting. She liked the feeling of not being in charge, of feeling feminine in his arms, safe yet free at the same time.

Regina arched as his talented tongue wriggled through the grasp of her vagina.

Mitch growled, his thoughts linking to hers. That name, Tobias. He wanted to know what this Tobias meant to her. His memory pulled no one on the base to mind. So he crossed a line he'd set for himself many years ago. If she found out that he'd gone through her memories without permission she'd never forgive him. Now his heart was in danger and he needed to know how close this Tobias was to the linguist in his arms.

He searched her mind for that focus. What he found there startled and angered him.

Tobias was the name of the lover who exploited her naivety. She had no idea who she hooked up with that night. No wonder she thought of him all starry-eyed. He watched the memory in her mind, but could not find anything that tied her to the one-night stand but incredible sex. Tobias treated her more like a brainteaser for lack of a better description.

Mitch watched her memory of that night, of Tobias, focused on them, like an unseen voyeur hanging in her memory. What a strange ménage, the thought flitted through his mind as he concentrated on doing both things well. Finding her secret lover and doing his best to erase the phantom and replace him.

What he witnessed was the sexual education of Regina, her awakening as a woman. He viewed them, listening to the other man reveal, show and enjoy the results of pleasures with her. She acted like a kid with a new game, her long fingered hands playing the places Tobias stroked. Her face glowed with carnal discovery, her bright eyes tearing with the passion blooming inside of her.

He found himself agreeing with the male, what kind of idiot had she married? All this untapped fire and passion waited for a lover to free it and a naval commander to validate it. He withdrew from her mind, keeping a soft touch there, gauging her reactions. One blunt finger and then two worked through her slick cream, opening the tight muscles of her cunt, preparing her for his invasion. He had no false modesty as far as his body was concerned. He was probably going to hurt her at first.

She was tight, almost virginal, and he wondered at her celibacy while in the facility. Since the one time lover woke her to her sensual side, he'd have thought she would burn through the men like a flash fire. Her self-control under those circumstances impressed him. Or she might have found the selection limited, like he did.

A long, low moan shifted his full attention to the woman in his hold. The other thought he pushed aside, the one that made them the same. The one he shared because he'd been looking for the one he'd given up on finding. And he'd been living beside her for months now.

Mitch teased her a little longer and then, before she reached another climax, he moved to enter her. *Shit, no protection.* He froze, his body throbbing like a toothache, balls tight to his body.

"Don't stop," she pleaded as she arched to bring her body back into contact with his heat.

"No condoms."

Panting breaths, the subtle glide of skin on fabric, the mattress sighing under the shifting weight settling on top, these sounds filled the incredible and sudden quiet of her bedroom. For a few moments she weighed the situation. Mitch didn't let her go completely, his hand stroked her stomach, gentling her. Regina did not want to come down. Finally she was free to play with another body and she was not giving it up. Chances of her getting pregnant were minuscule. Having finished her cycle a couple of days ago, there wasn't anything there to get them into trouble. Physical checks performed on anyone coming into the facility for blood borne illnesses assured no cross contamination, and since she had not returned topside for any amount of time, she was clean.

"Mitch, have you been topside?" Regina rolled to her side, dislodging his hand, but able to clasp his cock. Up on her elbow, she took him in hand, touching and stroking him. Mitch tried to move away, but her hand followed him, stimulating him back to fullness.

"No, I've kept *Below* the whole time I've been here, why?"

"We don't have anything transmittable, and I am not ready to get pregnant right now. Well, for the next two weeks or so, anyway."

"What are you telling me?" He wanted to know in black and white that no gray areas would exist that could come back to bite them.

"I'm saying we don't need protection. We are both clean, and I am not fertile. No need to stop, if you don't want to." Gods knew she didn't want to stop until he was balls deep, putting out the fire burning her alive.

He studied her, watched as her body fidgeted against his, rubbing and caressing skin to skin. Mitch wanted this woman now, if he could never have her again. He made his decision. In one movement he captured a handful of her rioting curls and rolled her body under his. One stroke opened her and stretched her slick heat around his cock.

Regina screamed. Her body bowed to take his. The flare of heat and pain as he stretched her for him destroyed her. Her body clenched in orgasm, riding the top from wave to wave as his cock shafted her harder, then deeper as her legs rose to grip him.

Mitch covered her scream, drinking in the elemental echo. His hand still wrapped in red curls moved her head, tilting her mouth to match his, fusing their lips in the deep kiss. His other hand held her hip, keeping her steady beneath his thrusts. Her breasts cushioned his chest, her nails scraped him bloody. Inside, a beast roared with pleasure, contentment, possession. He loved tearing her apart, forcing her around his body, stroking deep and deeper still until he reached bottom, his claim complete. The cool detached doctor became a raging virago who burned him alive with her fury. Her body labored with his, reaching for more, begging him to finish her, unleashing the last of his control.

Regina struggled to let him know what he was doing to her, but her gasps and pleading seemed to fall on deaf ears. She ached. Her body cramped around his solid length buried inside her, stroking places she'd never had stroked before. His big body drove her against the headboard. Pulling her hair added another layer of sensation to the conflagration flaring between them. She arched, trying to get him deeper, wanting him to split her open and crawl inside her body and soul. She shredded his back, not once realizing the damage or the sensual whip those scratches acted on Mitch.

When Mitch could take no more he grabbed her hands and forced them over her head. Clamping them together in his fist, he hooked her leg with his elbow, opening her further for his thrusts, the stroking of his long cock. His mouth dropped to hers, breath gusting on her lips.

"I need you, Regina. I need to fuck you, hard and deep." He spoke to her in a growl, his voice hoarse with desire.

"Yes, yes, yes." She forced her eyes open to see him. She tried to relax. Pleasure and pain twisted inside her, leaving a longing, a need only he could assuage now. She needed more, needed everything.

"You're mine." She managed to tell him, her voice unrecognizable. He belonged to her now. She watched his eyes flare with her words, a ruddy color seeming to bloom from within. His face screwed into a pained grimace, he locked his gaze with hers, holding her still beneath him.

He ratcheted his stroking up another notch, his hips a blur as he pumped his cock into her body, stretching and filling her. Her cream flowed between them, coating them both in the sea brine scent. The comforter absorbed the puddle. Still he rammed home, seating himself deep within her grasping cunt. He could feel the shocks from his balls to his brain, signaling the beginning of the end.

He leaned his body on hers. Taking his free hand and using his knuckle on her clit, he rubbed her, trying to be gentle, but ruthlessly forcing her laboring body into yet another orgasm. When Regina arched beneath him, her head back for air and her pussy open yet a grasping fist surrounding him, he let go. Filling her, pump after jetting pump, his cock emptied into her, coating her with his fluid, filling her with his essence and pouring his soul into her with every short-circuited buck of his body into hers.

He wanted more with her, more time, more of her body. He wanted to learn her mind, what she wanted, what she already knew. He would not allow the fact he was a soldier and she a doctor to divide them. Not now, reality would cloud this whatever they experienced soon enough. His mind locked and his gaze softened as he looked down at her. He'd claimed her and she'd marked him with blood. They belonged to each other. Somehow that was right with his soul, with the animal that stretched under his skin, the primitive animal brain agreed as it relaxed.

Regina breathed in relief as his orgasm flooded her, putting out the fire burning her from the inside. With a sigh, she acknowledged she wanted him to start the barely banked flames again. His body settled beside her on the bed, his straining chest beside her head. His hand relaxed his hold on hers. She finished freeing herself and turned to drape her sated body over his. She relaxed when his other arm curled around her, holding her fast to his side. Her hand rose to rake through his damp hair, twisting strands between her fingers. Her other hand glided across the wide expanse of humid skin, feeling the movement covering his laboring lungs. The forceful pounding of his heartbeat slowed. His nipples beaded in the coolness of her quarters, so she closed her lips over one, thinking to warm it.

Mitch jumped beneath her. She smiled and looked up to see him watching her play. She opened her mouth and licked the small aureole and the nipple brought erect with her actions as if she was licking an ice cream cone. She swirled her tongue as though capturing a dribble.

Mitch groaned and pulled her onto his chest, moving that dangerous organ away from his body. His cock surged damp against his thigh as she settled. "Woman, be still. I'm too young to die," he groused. He smiled up at her as she followed his order and made herself at home. One hand supported her chin so she could study him while her other hand caressed and left flickers of sensation along the side of his head from crown to shoulder.

"It's only fair. You killed me," she whispered, her blue gaze serious.

Mitch wanted to believe those words. Those blue eyes promised him forever, no shadows and no hidden agendas. She wanted him as much as he wanted her. In this cocoon of time they could have each other. The cold reality outside this door would not be so simple. A growl rose from his chest as he considered that feeling. The animal inside him claimed her. She would be his, she belonged to him, his woman, his mate, and nothing was going to keep them apart. In the cooling aftermath, reality eased in, separating them.

Regina watched as he slowly, reluctantly withdrew from her, from them. Fear filled her and she began the second guessing game with herself. As soon as her mind engaged the primal side of her, some Amazon throwback mentality surfaced. She would fight him, fight for him. With every weapon at her disposal she would make him see them, together. Did he even realize he stroked her from ass cheeks to shoulders as she sprawled across his body?

Reluctant to let her go, he held her to him. His heart, a pagan tattoo beating its rhythm into her body, slowly eased. His body and hers started cooling in the controlled environment. Regina was stuck to him. Maybe a shower would help. It would give them both a chance to internalize what just happened between them, a breather of sorts before the real world butted in.

At the edges of her consciousness life crouched, ready to flood them with decisions, hard decisions that would have to be made and choices that would affect the lives of ten other men. "Race you to the shower. Winner gets her back scrubbed by the loser, Loser." She twisted to get free.

"Not if I can help it." In a sudden burst of movement he rolled her to the comforter and grabbed the edge, whipping it around her as he shot out of bed. A feline snarl sounded behind him. His muscles stiffened by the unaccustomed exercise, he was slow getting around her bed to the bath. But he did get there first. He adjusted the water temperature to warm before she stormed into the enclosure. Her blue eyes blazed in her flushed face. A smile promising retribution curled her lips. He smiled back, answering her challenge. He stood on one side of the shower, letting her have the other two water heads. Closing his eyes, he relished the warm water flowing over him, drawing a curtain between what was and what would be. He was determined to enjoy her now. Later, well, they would have to wait to see what later brought.

The scratches she'd made burned, and a primeval leer of pride and arrogance curled his lips. He'd made her lose all that cool control. He rehashed the last hour or so, wanting to experience more of her. Taking a bar of soap, he lathered the sweat off his body, watching the suds circle the drain and disappear. Afraid in his gut that what they experienced would do the same, swirl away from them.

Chapter 9

A gasp brought his head up. His eyes searched the room for a threat. Too many years as a SEAL, too many days and nights deep in black ops like this one, honed his skills as a killer, a predator. He moved to her side of the shower, pulling her behind him, reaching out mentally to douse the lights. It all happened in a second.

He leaned to Regina's side, still keeping his bigger body between her and the door where a shaft of light entered the room.

"What is it?" The barest sound came from her over the rush of water.

"Oh, goddess forgive, Mitch. Your back is a mass of welts and bloody scratches," she whispered when she could talk.

The sudden reaction of his body to her startled gasp brought home what he was. Probably like all the rest of the military down here, he was a trained weapon. It all rushed back to her, the deaths, the danger, and the faces. She shuddered in the water, wishing it were set to scald, knowing the cold went deeper than her flesh.

"It's okay, really," he assured her, incorrectly guessing her distress. He turned the lights back up so they could find towels and get out. Once he saw her face it registered that she was shocky. Regina was fast heading for emotional overload. He could tell it in her voice, see the chaos in her mind. He watched her fine skin break out with chill bumps. Finding a towel, he wrapped her tightly in the material. Setting her aside for now, he grabbed another towel and, using a minimum of movement, got most of the water off himself for the third time today.

He lifted her in his arms and took her back to bed. Pulling the comforter and bedding down, Mitch rolled her out of the towel and between the soft sheets. Pulling them back over her shivering body, he settled beside her, on top of the linens. Layers between them kept his libido on hold, so far. He rubbed her back, watching her eyes as she assimilated the pandemonium in her head.

He listened in as her thoughts tangled, emotions blasting through rational concepts. Beliefs twisted with suspicions, he blinked when a pure thought rose through the maelstrom.

The self-knowledge that Regina believed she loved him. His thought processes ground to a halt. Every sense on automatic kept his heart beating, his lungs processing air.

Her hand shot out to take his, as though fearful he would leave her. Regina worked to categorize and compartmentalize the whirling issues banging around her tired brain. She held onto Mitch, a steady post in her life right now.

The blender of her mind slowed and stopped. Her hand gripped Mitch, holding him next to her. She surprised herself with the need for him. It was too soon to acknowledge her heart's involvement. It would scare him, because that silver lining surrounded a cloud of unknown, which scared her.

When he gathered her hair off her face the fine strands curled around his fingers with a life of their own as they dried.

"I'm sorry." Her apology was delivered by whisper, loath to break the fragile moment between them.

"Don't be." His gaze sought and held hers. "It's been quite an evening."

She watched as memories chased through his eyes, the good and the not so good. With her body temperature now normal, she pushed up to sit against the pillows.

"It's not over, you know." Her voice grew stronger while her eyes followed the contours of his chest and abdomen. The simple sentence had a wealth of meanings, all of them tangled.

Mitch absorbed the look like a touch. His body reacted to the invitation she broadcast. She rose from the bedding, her body already showing his incautious marks. He wanted to kiss each one, loving the dark blood filled spots marring her creamy skin. She wore his declarations with pride. She moved to him on her knees and turned his shoulders so she could look at his back. He smiled as Doc Reggie lightly touched her passion marks. With her touch cool, she strived to be professional, even as she caught her breath while she moved her hand over his skin.

"At least you don't need stitches," she told him, easing him back to face her. "I didn't know I was capable of that, Mitch. I know they must hurt." She stroked his jaw, moving her fingers over his lips in the same light touch she used examining his back.

"You bring me to violence," she admitted softly, her gaze lifting to meet his. "You make me forget everything but the way your body feels with mine, your strength, your size, the way you stretch me, fill me." She rose to his lap. "Something inside me roars to life, another being I'm not familiar with lives here." She pressed her hand to her heart as her legs wrapped around his waist, anchoring her to his body. Her words and actions brought his cock surging back to life. Having the same effect on her, settling on his body she shivered in primal reaction.

He pulled her deeper into him, her already slick pussy opened for him to enter her. Her head fell back as she accepted him. Her body bucked against his, struggling to take more of him inside. He stretched back on her bed, allowing her to ride him as deeply or shallowly as she wanted. His calloused hands grasped her thighs, holding her astride him.

Regina remembered riding Tobias, but he was nothing like the man beneath her now. She arched, opening herself wide for his possession, because that was what this was, his control of her body, mind and soul. Her hips lifted, her thigh muscles jumping with the strain and the pleasure of being so full. She gasped these half thoughts to him, working her body over him, straining for her release and the erotic force of pleasure ripping through her.

His body arched, allowing her fuller penetration, and that was all it took, the blunt head of his cock bumping the mouth of her womb, the pressure and heat of him deep inside. Regina gripped him with her thighs, her hands on her chest, rolling down on him, losing control with a scream as her body rocked on top of his.

Mitch rolled her underneath him, picking up the thrusting movements before her body finished with hers. He caught the orgasm, thrusting it back to her, creating a mindless feedback loop of pleasure in her he enjoyed. Filling her to the root of his cock and then some, he stroked her with long lunges. Before she could reach for him, her claws out for more of his blood, he rolled her to her stomach.

Bunching the covers under her gyrating hips, he slipped through her cream, again seating himself deeper, if possible, in her clenching pussy. He held her hips, controlling their movements, dominating their ecstasy. Reared back, he watched as her swollen lips accepted his length and girth. His pelvis slammed against her ass cheeks as his hands bit into her waist.

Her back bowed, while her hands clawed the bedding beneath her as he shafted her. His brain spiked, pleasure and pain combined rushed through his system, roaring down his spine and erupting from his cock. Regina's begging, crying, hoarse voice goaded his libido. He wedged an arm under her, lifting her body and using her weight to drive her deeper onto his cock. He locked her thrashing body to his as he emptied everything he had into her grasping sheath. His body arched back, his lungs laboring for air, his muscles trembling in release.

In time he lowered Regina to the bedding, settling his trembling body beside her. The ache in his head behind his eye pounded in the aftermath of their spent passions. He closed his eyes to try to wrestle the pain to a tolerable level. It spiked with every beat of his heart, making him smile in spite of the pain as his body relaxed beside Regina.

"We gotta eat," she mumbled without turning her head. Her body sprawled boneless alongside his soaked in his heat. It was a supreme effort to turn her head to him, too much work to open her eyes. so she kept them closed. Her hair was a Titian veil between them and she couldn't muster the energy to push it aside. "Or did you have a chance to grab something when you left the lab?"

"No." He stroked the sensuous line of her back. Slightly queasy with riveting pain, he wasn't hungry. "You called me out of the shower. I headed right over."

"Wonder what the cafeteria has tonight?" Regina moved so he could reach more of her back.

"Does it matter?"

"No." She rolled to face him, her eyes finally opening to see his flushed face. Concern shot through her. "What's wrong?"

"Damned headache, it'll pass in a few. Probably hunger," he lied to her. She believed him as her stomach rumbled. With a supple move she was off the bed and digging for clothes.

"I can fix that quickly," she told him as she pulled on yoga pants and a fitted top. He watched her dress, admiring her quick movements. The scratch of the top over her nipples caused them to rise under the plush abuse. He licked his lips, wanting thirds already.

"No need to rush," he murmured as lassitude swept through him. She fled the bedroom to return with his clothes in hand. He looked from them to her.

"Determined, aren't you." Moaning, he moved to take the clothes. Shaking them out, he sorted them and put them on. He slid his feet into his shoes and turned to watch as she headed back from the living room.

Her eyes slid quickly to the laptop, but no message waited for her. She took a deep breath and joined Mitch in the hallway.

They listened as the door locked behind them. She tucked her keycard into her pocket.

"Would you like to join me for a late meal?" Mitch asked her as they headed for the cafeteria.

"I would love to, Mitch." It was too early for public displays between them, but she hungered for his taste. A glance behind them showed nothing but empty corridor. She grasped his arm with one hand, pulling him toward her. Standing on tiptoe, she lightly nibbled his lips until he cupped her head and kissed her, tongue to tongue. She smiled, satisfied.

Mitch pulled her along toward food. If she was going to keep this level of intensity up, he needed more fuel. He glimpsed her thoughts, smiling as he acknowledged she wanted to keep this going all night. He was gonna need take out after dinner.

Mitch walked the corridors in the early morning. Not that anyone knew time of day *Below*. He'd spent the bulk of the night riding Regina and enjoying her rides. His body dragged from the pleasure, while his mind worked double speed. His name topped the list for final injections next week, then the light treatment. He thought of the men already in the studies, the first two teams murdered. What would happen to the last group of guinea pigs with him? Troubled by the lack of concrete evidence, his hopes on the messages he'd sent earlier, he strode into his quarters and looked at his laptop.

The notification light on the side of his keyboard blinked. He hoped it was solid information he could use. He settled in the darkness and opened his email.

Reading his messages took some time. Some of them he read repeatedly. Sources reported to him on the validity of the friendly fire, but there seemed to be a part of the story missing. Had something happened to all test subjects that precipitated their extermination? He printed off the emails to hardcopies, deleting all traces from his computer. Taking the copies, he placed them in a file and locked them in his safe.

He'd wished to have more information, but the answers he'd received left him with more questions. With questions he needed answers to, time was running away from him.

He had an hour before breakfast and time to report to training. Mitch debated taking a nap, but he headed to the shower instead. He was getting used to their mingled scents on his body and hated washing them off. The promise to himself that he would spend the night with Regina tonight got him into the shower. He had to have some space from her to find the brooding officer everyone expected. Reporting with a sappy smile would undo the myth he built around himself.

He also needed to come to terms with every rule he and Regina had broken in the last eight hours. He wanted her, that he could admit. He was emotionally involved in that she was part of the experiment that killed so many other men who had no family. Was Regina alone? He hadn't asked her when they were together. The subject hadn't surfaced. They'd been busy satisfying other needs.

She wasn't a love-'em-and-leave-'em woman. What she felt was deep and solid. He gritted his teeth, his jaw tight as a shiver ghosted over him at her thoughts of love. She looked for a forever, and he had another week. If he survived there would be another mission, another op he would lead or be part of, and he would leave her behind.

He wasn't sure if he loved her, an emotion foreign to him. Protective, yes he was very protective. Attracted? Hell, yes. He wanted her so much now that his cock rose as he washed the dried residue off his thighs. But he had no promises of tomorrow. He would have to make her understand before they were too deep.

Dressed in dungarees for training, he headed for the cafeteria to join the team. He wanted a little face time with each of them before letting them loose for the day. Maybe he could discover some side-effect or glitch in the serum the mad scientist had overlooked. He wanted to find something to defer the testing and aid the release of his team. Since the last teams met certain death, he would protect this bunch with every loophole he could find.

He sat among his team. Everyone seemed in high spirits and more than ready to go forward. In a bubble of worry, Mitch listened to the joking and playing, thinking of the others who had no one to mourn them. He didn't want these to join their fellow soldiers.

Regina started her day hours later. She didn't leave for the lab until after oh-seven-hundred, a little late because she'd examined every bite, every hickey on her body. Standing in front of the mirror in her room, she'd found every imprint of Mitch's mouth. Like Cinderella, her midnight had come and gone, leaving her with the memory of the best night of her life.

Doubts followed the euphoria. The last eight hours contradicted on so many levels. Both her employment forbid any relationships within the scope of the project, especially with a subject. She dressed for work, trying to talk her heart out of loving him. When that didn't work, she switched to convincing her mind. With little better luck, she understood that last night was a fluke, a surprise that answered a need brought on by shock at the betrayal of her work. Her brain told her that he was an officer, no less a gentleman for marking her body with high school claims. He had a life after this set of trials. He had a command to return to, a life that didn't include her.

Unable to win any peace of mind over the conundrum of the budding relationship and blooming love, she left her apartment.

The latest lot of serum waited for verifying before the next set of injections. She focused on testing by rote. Her mind constantly slid through her actions and reactions of last night. Noting no variations in the batch, she sent the latest reports to the mad scientist through email.

Seriously compromised by her inattention in the lab, by lunch she needed to escape. Back in her quarters, she finished some of the take-home food they'd gotten last night. She straightened the rooms, took out her trash, tried to relax. The faint scent of sex still perfumed the air. Regina found she had to escape her rooms. The only other option was to go back to the lab. Before leaving she filled a workout bag and took it back with her. Some strenuous exercise would take her mind off the coming night and the hope Mitch would return.

Neither of them had made any commitments last night, and when she woke this morning it was to an empty bed, the sheets cold, the pillow dented where Mitch had slept with her.

Getting to the lab, she opened the door to find Dr. Laurel there. Tracy shot her a relieved glance, the normally unflappable technician stood back from her station while Dr. Laurel peered into her monitor.

"Good afternoon, Dr. Laurel. What brings you to our lab?"

Regina dropped her bag inside the door of her office. She approached the station.

"Good afternoon, Regina." He always called her by her name. It used to bother her, but not anymore. She'd gotten over his condescending manner early on. He'd never tacked on her doctorate. She watched as he straightened and slid his glasses back up his nose.

"I wanted to check your last couple of test runs on the serum. I seem to be developing an issue with the cocktail in combination with my findings." He moved to another computer station, the one she worked with while testing. Her morning results were still there. Regina watched him mutter as he checked her data.

"Where is the issue developing?" She moved to him, looking over his shoulder. If she got him talking maybe he'd let something slip. Mitch discovered the mad scientist was covering up the outcome of the first two teams. She'd looked over this batch herself a few hours ago. Every test was within the working parameters set up for them.

While she was convinced the serum matched every other batch of the hundreds of batches cooked in the lab in the weeks and months since she had deciphered the recipe, she waited for his endorsement.

"We make no substitutions, all ingredients are coming from confirmed sources above ground and everything is pharmaceutical grade." Regina straightened behind him. "I don't understand."

"I don't, either. I have gone through my stores, mixing them according to the original research." Dr. Laurel turned to her, his eyes fixed on some middle ground she could not see.

"Let's go back, each team, to the original way we did these combinations. It could be something as simple as temperature changes causing a decrease in the effectiveness." He turned and left muttering. Regina thought she heard him say, *or increase the effectiveness* before he left the lab. She exchanged a look with Tracy. Her tech shrugged, unable to add anything to what Regina just witnessed.

She wasn't about to head for the promised workout now. It seemed she needed to look into her end of the experiment in more detail than she'd previously done. With the secret of the preceding teams' deaths burning inside her stomach, she took a deep breath and looked around.

Worried that something she was doing was ultimately the cause of twenty deaths and more if it wasn't fixed, she immediately directed

Tracy to pull up all records from two years ago, starting with animal testing.

"We need all records from the start day. There must be something there we're missing."

Tracy nodded and moved to her computer. "If it's our fault-"

"Don't think it," Regina told her, knowing Tracy's relationship with Adams. Like her burgeoning connection with Mitch, they worried about their men. Regina more, because she hadn't disclosed the friendly fire episode with anyone. It was better for Tracy not to know, she reasoned, keeping her lips sealed even as the need to tell her friend rose to fill her mouth.

"If it's in the serum we'll find it." She turned back to her screens. "If it exists farther down the line we'll help fix it."

She pulled her chair under her, turning her full attention to research and finding those files and purchase orders on her supplies. If the mad scientist was concerned, maybe he had heard of the deaths as well. She wanted to believe Dr. Laurel was innocent, but Mitch's suspicions cast him in a darker light, one she had trouble dismissing.

Chapter 10

Countless hours later, long after she told Tracy to go home, Regina rubbed her eyes, once more attempting to focus on the screen in front of her. Reading the print was almost impossible with her brain so tired. Researching the whole methodology from concept to completion had taken all day and into the night. Regina studied the transfer of the lab and ingredients. Since all items were easier to control *Below*, Regina studied until she could track every change in temperature to the tenth of a degree.

The purchase orders she scanned and double-checked, including the alphanumeric identifier of each batch. When the seasons changed, she'd personally checked the raw materials shipped to them. Dried herbs were very forgiving, but moisture could change their state.

As each batch was vacuum packed and sealed, only the current bag was opened when the next batch of serum called for it. There was no way those herbs were contaminated. The water, purified for her lab, still checked out to have the same concentrations of trace elements as two years or more ago. She and Tracy, then her next shift techs, Mike and Amelia, pulled samples of materials, cleaning supplies, sterilization chemicals, everything she could possibly see affecting any aspect of the finished product were thoroughly examined. Repeatedly she tested, making sure she was not in any way responsible for a contaminated sample making its way to any human.

Mitch left his office late, or early, depending on how one perceived it it. He'd gotten word out and assurance there would be an investigation. Greg had cautioned him to be careful. He didn't deny the killings, but he didn't go into any detail, either. The general's voice had held a note that seemed more than personal, as though he hid some information from Mitch. Mitch didn't question his cousin, assuring him he was doing all he could to find the issue.

Mitch got so busy with reviewing the lists of his conversations with each of his men, that he hadn't realized how late, or early it had become. He stretched, wondering if Regina was asleep. Luckily, it was Friday or Saturday morning by now, since *Below* took their weekends off. Turning his office lights off and locking the door behind him, he headed for the cafeteria. The activity stimulated his hunger.

The cafeteria was empty but for two people, since the night shift already finished with their lunch break. He'd missed dinner and time with Regina, but surely she understood work could carry over from the usual shift.

He listened to the two others argue. Mike, the tech had explained the serum to him what seemed so long ago and the other tech who worked with Regina were going at it.

"There is nothing wrong with the work." Amelia held Mike's forearm. She leaned into him, insisting.

"There's something. The mad scientist was searching for a glitch in the research, formulation, or process." Their hushed whispers stopped when Mike noticed Mitch stepping up to their table.

"What's happening?" Clear authority rang through his question, so the techs didn't hesitate to answer him.

"It's the mad scientist," Mike told him, dislodging the hold Amelia had on his arm and leaning back in his chair. "He's looking for something but not telling us what. We delved into every batch of serum, every animal test and everything works exactly as it's supposed to." He ticked off each statement on his fingers in emphasis. "He's been in every computer in the lab, taking over Doc Reggie's this afternoon and looking through her notes." Throwing up his hands, he sighed, rubbing bloodshot eyes.

"There's absolutely nothing wrong with the work we've done. I don't get it. It's like he's missing some reaction he's looking for, so the fault is ours because the serum isn't suddenly acting like he wants it to."

Amelia drew Mitch's attention. "Doc Reggie has a bug up her ass, calling us in to research the research and test the recipes all over again. She's thinking there is something wrong with the serum. We've been working with her for hours and she's still not satisfied all is well."

Mitch believed all of the techs who worked with Regina loved her. Each one of them was unswervingly loyal to her, so to find half her team frustrated with her was a surprise

"She's just being careful." Mike finished the last swallow of pale tea with a grimace.

"She's being a pain in the ass," Amelia snapped back. Exhaustion had taken its toll.

"What else would you be doing if not going back over the testing and recipes?" Mitch asked.

Amelia shook her head. "Exactly. We've been chillin' and now it's time to work. It'll be over soon enough and we'll be back hunting for work topside."

Mike got to his feet, tray in hand. "You coming back?"

Amelia nodded with a sigh. "I just don't get it. She's like a mad woman hunting for the proverbial needle." She gathered her tray and walked behind Mike to dispose of the trash.

Mitch watched them go. Regina, if he believed their story, was harder at work than he'd been. Both of them were trying to find the key to unlocking this nightmare they'd discovered.

As time dragged on, it became her greatest fear that she'd somehow risked the lives of her human volunteers. Punishing images of those personalities filtered through her determination, bringing tears to her eyes. Every memory strengthened her resolve, driving her beyond exhaustion to find the answers buried in the body of work. If it was in the serum, she would find it.

Again she reviewed the lab specimen results, going over every recorded meal, blood test, bowel movement, looking at footage as the animals slept, their chests rising and falling in regular rhythm. All animal testing was fully recorded and everything checked out. Everything looked good with every trial, every note, and every temperature.

Sometime around three o'clock she'd dismissed her team. They were getting on each other's nerves, getting in each other's way, driving her crazy with distractions. They were tired and hungry, and she couldn't blame them.

She'd added to their stress, asking them to check and double-check all the records of every moment they'd worked on this project. She had to be certain the problem hadn't come from her work or her workers. More subjects were heading down the same dead end path as the others. She watched films of each set of animals. Every single time their recorded reactions were the same. She went into the kennels, still studying the animals they kept as controls. Some slept, some socialized, and none of them displayed any adverse reactions. None of them received any of her serum anymore.

She accessed public records of Dr. Laurel's studies as they dovetailed with hers. Brooding over the texts, she tried to find a flaw with his logic. As a research biologist, she understood setbacks. She had had a few, even with finding the correct measurements for this potion. She sighed and blanked her computer, closing window after window. She needed some down time. Her brain whirled with possibilities to explore, though her checklist had marked them as complete. She dreaded the walk back to her quarters. Tired in spirit and body, she told herself to rest a minute and then head for bed. In a moment, she would drag her aching body home, in a few...

Mitch found her in the lab after he'd checked her apartment three times in as many hours. He'd searched the gym and the pool. She hadn't been seen in the cafeteria. Frustrated, he'd stalked to Tracy's quarters. He rang the bell. The door slid open. .A completely disheveled Tracy blinked at him.

She gazed at him from toe to brow, shaking her head and leaning farther out into the hall. Looking right and left, she turned back to stare up at Mitch. "Can't find her?"

Mitch shook his head at her drowsy question.

"Lab."

"Hey, Trace. Getting lonely." Mitch recognized the voice, so he nodded and turned to leave.

"Hey, glad she finally gave in." Tracy's whisper carried him back to the laboratory hall. He was a grown man fighting the need to express the overwhelming need to roar his possessiveness to the world that she belonged to him. The whisper made him smile, the burden he carried lightened. He wasn't the only one to find happiness in the bowels of the earth. He walked into the open lab with his need to take care of a mate rising to the fore of his brain.

When Regina didn't seem to hear him, he took a moment to study her. She was a lean woman whose curves had slimmed down to almost nothing. She needed regular food, and a full night's sleep wouldn't hurt. He had a moment to wonder if she knew she was getting the same shots he and his team were. Was her sex making the changes starker? Could her body take the stresses this berserker serum would cause? His team worked out every day and some of them hit the gym in down time.

Regina worked out as sporadically as she ate. She swam a good bit, and she often snacked without eating a full meal. He'd been keeping an eye on her since he began to suspect the mad scientist had managed to include the fairer sex in his studies. Why create a berserker scientist? Why did there have to a woman? Why was it his woman? Those were more questions he'd love to get the answers to, even if he had to beat them out of the lying weasel in charge of this operation. His stomach rumbled.

He knew she kept her fridge clean, so there would be nothing to eat at her apartment. She sighed in her sleep, a little growl of a snore, her hands fisted. He frowned at her troubled sleep. She'd raked her hands through her hair so often in the hours it was a tangled mess around her shoulders. His hands itched to grab a brush and tame the snarls, gentling her from this madness that claimed her tonight.

"Regina?" He softened his voice, but the hard edge of his tone stirred. The emotions were not aimed at her, but at the circumstances surrounding them. It had been a long day for him, and this was clear evidence she was still working. Although work tomorrow was cancelled, he'd made sure the mad scientist understood they had one more day to absorb their changing conditions. He blamed the stay on their psychic needs. Laurel accepted, disgruntled, but would not go against the officer in charge. Mitch did have some power down here.

"Yes." She didn't look up from the scope she leaned on, as though her delicate neck couldn't support her head. He couldn't tell for a moment if she still slept or was actually awake.

The urgency of her work littered the lab in stacks of hardcopy. Some still rested on the printer tray. He left most of it, taking those pages he saw that contained information others shouldn't be privy to and stacking them in a pile before putting them in her desk.

Mitch knew her morning team would be in soon and the veterinary assistants would feed the zoo. They could take care of the rest of it. He pocketed her keycard after removing it from her hand. He curbed his smile as he stepped out of the locked office. Triumphant at winning that round, he wasn't about to push for more.

"The work day is over." He approached her workstation, only clasping her shoulders when she looked up and blinked. He didn't think she knew he was there, since she was buried in her thoughts.

The eyepiece had left an indent on her face, she'd pressed so tightly to the microscope looking for the mystery. And then she'd fallen asleep on the black rubber ring.

"I was checking the efficacy of the serum. It is as good as every other batch ever made. There should be no reason this is causing a decrease or increase in aggression in the men."

Mitch stiffened. Having just been asleep, she was clear and concise in her answer.

"There has been an increase of the aggression?"

"It seems the mad scientist believes so. I've been searching but can't find anything wrong." She shook her shoulders free of his hold. "It must be something he's doing. I've combined every cleaning agent, every temperature gauge. I can't find it."

"You're too tired now to see it. Tracy will be back in the morning, she can look. You need rest."

"The trials start tomorrow. I need to know it's safe." Every fear sounded in her terse words. He knew it was what drove her beyond exhaustion. It kept her checking every dust particle from receipt to delivery until her face was pale and her eyes bloodshot.

"It is, or I wouldn't be here." When he shook her the long bangs fell over her eyes. The glimpse he'd gotten showed him determination in her gaze, but exhaustion had carved deep purple hollows under her lashes.

"It's what killed the other teams."

"It isn't." Mitch looked around them. "Is there anything you need to shut down?"

"No."

"Then I'm taking you home."

"But I was checking—"

"And tomorrow you can finish." When she resisted he bent down and swept her knees into the crook of his arm. "You need to rest. When did you eat last?"

Not bothering to put up even a token fight, Regina let her head sag to his chest. "I had lunch."

"Not according to the cafeteria. No one saw you today."

"Leftovers."

Mitch snorted and turned to the outer lab office.

"Not hungry."

He smiled grimly. "I know. That's why we're going to eat." She weighed nothing in his arms. "And then to bed."

"I could set up the next chapter of material—"

"You will rest."

She let the anger at his highhanded attitude give her strength to struggle against his secure hold.

He finally put her down on her feet.

"I'm not one of your soldiers to order around."

"When you don't listen to reason—"

"That's bullshit. Reason is finding the cause of death," Frustration laced her tone. "stopping this madness before it claims more lives."

Patience wasn't his strong suit, but he crossed his arms and listened to her. Watching as she swayed on her feet, he gritted his teeth but kept his lips over them so she wouldn't see the snarl forming. Inside his head the strengthening animal instinct roared out, making him want to grasp her with clawed hands and force her to cooperate.

He took in a deep breath, forcing the brutal feelings down. Opening his arms, he took the half step to gather her to his body. He hugged her close, resting his chin on her head where she fit against him.

"You need rest and food. You are tired, and exhausted people miss things." He'd attack her defenses in another way. "You are barely keeping on your feet. I bet if you hadn't gotten angry at me you'd have fallen on your face." He pushed her back a bit. "Let me take care of you. You have taken care of us for so long."

"You suck." He was the calm voice of reason and she couldn't fight what he pointed out that she already knew. She was at the end of her rope physically. When she turned in his hold and started forward her stomach rumbled, answered by his. Time to eat, rest. Her body warmed beside his, his scent and strength so very appealing to her.

Needing to hold her, the animal inside him wouldn't be stopped. He scooped her into his arms again, where the warm bundle of woman fit perfectly. It wasn't love they felt for each other, but they needed to talk. He glanced down at his armload. She was already asleep.

Chapter 11

He walked slowly as she dozed in his arms. The sleeping bundle sighed and curled closer to his heat. Her lips moved and the softest sound escaped. He heard his name clearly. The smile escaped his control.

He hated to wake her, but she would sleep better on a full stomach. He'd always heard that. He moved her weight in his arms, pulling her up for a kiss.

"Sleep is for sissies," he whispered in her ear. Her lashes fluttered, one side of her mouth kicked up in the slightest smile.

"Time to eat, Doctor."

"Told you I'm not hungry." She squirmed in his arms, a sinuous move that had him thinking of things other than food. She broadcast the suddenly naughty thoughts to him as she roused his body. She did it on purpose, as if she knew he was a breath away from taking her any time they were together.

"Got to eat to have strength." He let his arm straighten slowly, allowing her to slide down his frame a slow inch at a time. By the time her feet hit the floor, she was awake and he was in pain. She leaned into his body, making it so wonderfully worse.

"What's on the menu?" Her hands ran up his thighs while she distracted him with her breathy question. Brain misfiring, Mitch gaped at her, wanting her hands higher, knowing food had to be the first order of business. He nodded and she chuckled, the sound husky and amazing. He was hard his back teeth ached, his balls tightened, and the wet spot grew at the head of his cock.

"We need to eat." Put that way she should get the hint. He sighed and leaned his back against the wall as her hands pulled away, along with her body heat. Taking a full breath, he straightened and ran a hand through his hair. He took another, dragging in the cooler air.

"Not funny." He pushed away from the wall and opened the door. Regina smiled at him, her features flushed and a smile dancing on her lips. That blue gaze slipped down his body coming to rest on the bulge of his cock pressing impatiently against his zipper. Her pink tongue ran over her lips. She backed to the doors of the cafeteria, teasing him. Then her superior attitude crashed as soon as she smelled food. Her stomach growled loud enough Mitch heard it from behind her.

With a gentle hand, he guided her to a line, getting plates and tucking wrapped silverware into a pocket for them both. Silence hung between them until they picked a table in mid room. Mitch left her and returned with drinks, setting four glasses between them. Regina hadn't waited, she was already eating her meal with single-minded purpose.

He shook out the napkin, palmed the silver and started on his meal.

He was still smiling when he swiped her card and opened the door of her quarters. She was definitely dreaming of him. His ego wondered what they were doing in her dream. He eased her to the bed, and then he wondered why he bothered. A herd of wild horses running by would not wake her. He stripped and turned down the bed before wrestling her clothes off. When he had her stripped, he rolled her body under the linens. After turning off all the lights but one, he slid his tired body in beside hers.

It would be a short night, but they both needed some sleep. He'd set the phone alarm to give them three and a half hours.

Pulling her to him, he listened to her soft breathing in the semi darkness. He was content holding her near. She eased his mind, body and soul. There were avenues he had yet to explore, but that was a worry for later. As her body warmed beside his, her soft breathing lured him into slumber. He adjusted his arm, not too tight or too loose below her breasts. He gave in and relaxed, letting sleep claim him.

Mitch dreamed of a beast, a great red beast. Huge, with wings as long as a tractor-trailer combination and a body almost as long, the animal searched for something. His great mouth opened, roaring into the clear sky, a clarion call, a male calling his female. Air lifted him, giant wings beating him away from the earth, carrying him up to meet his mate.

A smaller version of the red beast stroked alongside him, her sleek blue head snaking along his neck. The female was not his striking red, but a calming mosaic of blue/green. She glided, smaller wings helping her aerobatics. Her body coasted beneath his, her horned head struck his chest, her tail wrapped around his, holding her body against his great form.

He roared again, a clear threat to anything else in the sky. He loved the sinuous movements of his mate beneath him. He tried to still the instinct to clasp her to him, enter her and tumble through the sky until the hunger she raised in him was sated. She dropped away from him, teasing him yet. He reached for her, following her up into the sky, her sleek body luring him higher and higher. The temperature dropped against his scales before she allowed him to capture her, he locked them together, body wrapped around body.

He entered her, loving the desperate clasp of her body around his. Her body accepted his, welcoming him as deeply as possible. He folded his wings back, allowing them to free fall toward the earth. She held him with her limbs, her wings folded back, as well. Her neck curled around his in supplication. He locked her tighter, his body rushing to finish. Her soft roar in his ears let him know she was already coming as she stiffened. He consented and filled her body with his fluid, hastily managing to dislodge her so they could use their huge wings to slow their plummet. He roared his satisfaction to the sky.

Regina listened to the roar bounce off the walls of her bedroom. The dream left her shaken, the noise woke her up. She rolled to find Mitch in her bed, his sleepy gaze staring back at her.

"I had the most amazing dream." They'd shared the same dream.

Regina didn't know how much coffee later, she and Mitch sat in her living room, cradling cups still steaming, trying to make sense of the dream. By now each of them realized the dragons soaring through the sky represented them. It would be easy to dismiss it, except both of them had experienced the wonder of the dream. Another mystery, she sighed. This one was compelling, but the pressing order of business was saving the lives of the team.

She needed to get to the lab, restart her searching for anomalies in the serum itself. That meant her zoo was going to get active again. She needed to alert her vets, the caging arrangements would have to change, and the subjects would be placed in quarantine. There was a lot of work for them to set up for testing.

When she'd showered and dressed, she called the team and sent them ahead to create a batch of new serum and start the injections. It wasn't fair she was taking time with Mitch leaving them to work alone. She did not want to leave him. His time here was short, and if they couldn't solve the mystery around this experiment, it might be over. She refused to think of that, needing to believe the solution would come to them with enough hard work.

The thought of his bullet-ridden body, buried or cremated, sickened her. She would not allow the trial if that was to be the outcome. She would fight the government on this to keep more innocents alive. It would mean the loss of her income and likely the loss would follow her back to the civilian side of her profession. She'd be black-balled and ridiculed. She sighed.

"You are very far away from this room." Mitch interrupted her depressing thoughts. He had watched the different expressions chase across her face. He moved on the couch, putting his empty cup on the table. She looked up at him, her eyes red, grieving without tears.

With a quiet sob, Regina launched herself into his ready arms. Her cup forgotten in her rush, Mitch caught it, rescuing the glass and keeping them dry. Her body curled into his, her sobs came for the depths of her grief. Not the grief he'd felt from her, but fear. He eased her onto his lap, holding her as she struggled to get back under control.

"I won't let them have you," she swore in a low voice. He smiled.

"Regina, you have no control. I take orders from higher up, same as you. But I swore that I would take them, while you signed a contract. I have to follow this through. The only saving grace is that you trusted me and called me when you got the video. It means a lot that you turned to me before you turned your colleague, the mad scientist." He stroked her back. She had her face tucked against his chest. It felt natural holding her like this, natural to slide into bed beside her, pulling her against his body and falling asleep. He wanted this he admitted to himself. He wanted her forever. Now that he found her, he stood to lose her and so much more.

He seduced her, engaging her mind in love play, the actions rusty he used them so rarely. Her body had followed, towing her heart. He knew what filled her mind, the weak denials, and the strong voice of commitment. He eventually filled her body with his, their silky fluids mixing and scenting the air. This wasn't over, by a long shot. He rested with her sleeping dreamlessly in his arms.

It looked like both of them were going to be late today. He had no idea of the time, turned away from Regina's alarm clock. He stared at the ceiling. Soft light from the bathroom allowed him to see. The hard beating of his heart echoed in the darkness, a bass mutter to Regina's soft mewing. She dreamed of difficult things and he had no way to shield or protect her. The heavy beat thrust muscle against his ribs. He tried to adjust his position, easing the tapping. When there was no better posture, he forced himself to doze off, alert to her every sigh.

"The serum will be injected three days in a row, measured doses for weight. The reason for three days will be to build the herbs in your body. One dose is so small that you can metabolize it before it can enter your tissues. The transference of the herb through the epithelial cells will take a day, covering your entire body with the advance notice of a build-up. The third dose will activate your body from ready into overdrive. As soon as you feel anything different from your usual reactions to situations, report back here immediately." Regina looked every man in the eye as she explained this to them. Her reluctance to continue showed, but her orders were orders, binding as Mitch's.

Dr. Laurel moved forward to have his lecture with them. Regina stood at the labeled serum syringes, one loaded for every man here.

She reached for a stack of files, current blood pressures and temps on all eleven men about to enter the last testing phase. She'd been through them several times this morning, looking for whatever Laurel wanted from the experiment. She couldn't find anything different.

The biceps muscle in her arm pulled when she lifted the pile of folders to her chest, but she smiled. She'd finally managed to get Dr. Laurel to move the vitamin shot to her shoulder, instead of her neck. Yes, it pulled now. By this afternoon it would be forgotten, plus, no more bruised stomach.

Regina counted the files and the serum, making sure the doses were correct for weight on each file. She quieted and stood next to her techs, all of them ready to help her inject the class. She fought to keep her eyes straying to Mitch.

He'd stayed with her the weekend. They'd kept to themselves in her apartment. There had been talks, and sharing, and sex. The missing element was any thought of tomorrow. With the other two teams dead, neither ventured too closely to the probable outcome for this team.

Regina started thinking that tomorrow was a lot closer than she knew. Maybe she could make plans that included him. Maybe he wanted to be with her as much as she wanted to be with him. They'd talked so much, bundled together in her bed, or sprawled out on her couch.

By unspoken consent, neither of them talked about the trials.

Now was too late, the mad scientist was finished and the techs were lining everyone up in order. The harsh scent of alcohol stung her nose as the first of the injections started. She watched carefully to make sure the serum levels matched the calculated doses for each man. She double-checked herself before swabbing the first arm and pushing the plunger.

A part of her still smiled and joked with the men filing past her, some rubbing the injection sight, some wincing, all of them excited.

She swiped alcohol on the next arm, his scent a permanent part of her memory. She checked the dosage against his file, making sure everything was correct. She winced as the needle pierced his flesh, flesh she had kissed, licked and bitten over the long hours they spent together. When the plunger hit bottom, she could feel his body now working to connect all the players deep inside. He was the last man to exit the room.

Regina supervised the cleanup and disposal of all biological materials, now considered hazardous because of the blood and serum. It was business as usual, the third and final team of trials had started. She wondered if the mixed bag of psi scores would help this team or hurt them. It was something she would make note of in her journal, not a variable she wanted to include in public notes or emails.

Back in her lab, she checked the cooler where the next doses of the serum were stored. Temperature was fine, no fluctuations, no changes in color, or thickness. She locked the cooler, making sure no one could tamper with the next doses. Making the notations on the files, she finished the work in her office and headed for home and Mitch.

Chapter 12

When the time for the third injections arrived she was a wreck. Her emotions trapped on a coaster, she rolled from high to low in a matter of seconds. Rational thought was a shadow in the background, trying to get back to her. Never had she let subjects in a trial affect her so.

Never had she been in love, and that was the sole cause of her misery. No matter how she looked at it, no matter the information Mitch showed her, no matter the care she took with her end of the experiments, she held herself responsible for each life. Now she was possibly condemning the man she loved to certain death.

She and Mitch spent every possible hour together, hidden inside the relative sanctuary of her rooms. She worried as much as Mitch allowed, but he removed those thoughts with his body. Coming together was sweet and savage by turns. His needs overpowered her at times, leaving her breathless and hanging on to consciousness. Pushing their bodies to breaking to still the questions in their minds took their toll. Aside from brief naps often troubled by nightmares, they slept little.

Her fridge was stocked for the first time since she'd moved in. They shared the cooking duties to fuel their bodies. It passed the time and fed them balanced meals. The calories they burned up in her bed, on her couch, in the shower.

She'd whispered her love to him last night after she pushed them both so hard he finally succumbed to exhaustion, falling deeply asleep. Her body ached this morning. Everything touched off her temper. Her techs gave her a wide berth. She'd tried earlier to rebuild things between them, but it was not to be, not today.

Even Tracy, her true barometer, kept her distance since she'd snapped at them this morning over such a minor infraction. She'd forgotten the cause.

All she had to do is get through this and then watch for the men to start trickling in one or two at a time, like with every other trial.

She was strong enough to get through this. She had to be. The room emptied, like on the previous mornings. The excitement ratcheted up to a feverish pitch in all the men. Each man there knew that today he would become the next generation of the military's greatest weapon. All were eager to be the brand new next-gen soldiers in the war against terrorism. Their locker room antics couldn't make her smile.

Mitch took his shot, like the rest. There would be a down period, and then all gathered in the gym to work in various wavelengths of lighting. The most aggression appeared in low light situations, the ruddy glow of dawn or dusk stimulated the berserker rage the mad scientist was looking for.

Once the energized soldiers left the room, silent through their last instructions, Mitch went to his quarters. He'd asked for something to be shipped to him. Not allowed mail, he'd had it delivered to a local PO Box, then asked Tracy to pick it up for him.

She returned with it, handing it over with a cat and canary grin.

"No word."

She made an X over her heart. "I promise. When will you tell her?"

"When it's time."

The excitable bundle pulled him down and kissed his cheek. "She'll be so happy. Congratulations."

He hoped it worked out.

If she followed her routine she would be looking through the files in her small office off the lab. It was quiet there and she used the solitude to collect her thoughts. He opened the door and a soft footfall brought him to her. Unerringly he found her trying to lock herself away from what she feared was going to happen.

Mitch watched her behind her desk. She used it as a shield today, to keep everyone away. Her hand rubbed her shoulder absently. It must be bothering her. He moved to her, settling on her desk, blocking her monitor. She didn't move for a moment, then she shot to her feet, escape on her mind. His hand shot out, clasping her forearm and halting her flight. He pulled her to him, settling her between his thighs. Taking the lab coat off her shoulders, he tossed it to her chair. Lifting her short sleeve, he looked at the arm she rubbed. There and there were tiny punctures, surrounded by telltale bruises. His conjecture was correct. Like all of them, for whatever twisted reason remained, the folks who funded this research wanted the results on a female as well as the males. He didn't know if the end was living or dead.

"You are part of the study, I see." His voice hard, he was disgusted that he couldn't have stopped it.

Regina lifted her head, looking at him. Immediate denial flared in her eyes.

In the intellectual storm that followed, he watched and listened to her mind as she put together all the things he'd realized some time ago.

No one else was taking vitamin injections. She'd asked casually around of her staff. All along, she'd been groomed like the rest of the men. Two injections into the serum, she was in the delicate balance between being ready and being finished.

"He told me it was to bolster the vitamins because smaller doses were being injected into my arm instead of my neck or stomach."

"He lied."

"I see how it must look." Regina studied the second button on his BDU shirt. Mitch waited for her, knowing she had to accept the truth. She was in denial, not ready to face the same death that could happen to her last team. She was too late into the schedule to back out. Whatever the serum was going to bring about in the men, the same thing was going to happen to her, even if she didn't take the last injection.

"I'm scared." Her tearful gaze met his, her face paled more than he'd thought it could. He didn't hesitate to pull her into a warm hug. The thrashing of his heart, growing stronger as the days of serum passed, tapped against her chest. The heavy beat seemed to stutter against her, not regular yet faster as if it were a double beat.

"I know it, Regina." She absorbed the strength of him, finding the anger she'd need to get through this. "I listen to it as you dream. I hear it in your voice. The stress comes out in the way you work with your team, pushing them away from you." He pulled her tighter against him. "You're isolating yourself from those who care for you."

"Aren't you scared?" Her voice came as a mere whisper, as though she feared insulting him. Inside of her the anger twisted, a live animal waiting for release. A shiver moved through her as sweat sheened her brow. There was a twisting, an urge under her skin to break free to find a cool spot.

"I have you to watch over me."

The bomb inside of her exploded. "I'll kill him, the lying son of a bitch," she exploded. Her back ramrod straight, she twisted her arm to see the signs of injection. Thrusting out of his arms, she growled between clenched teeth. Inside her, the being that inhabited her moved sinuously, pressing against the prison that was her flesh.

"I'm not getting the daily shots like the men. I get these weekly. At least that is how often I was told I needed the *vitamins.*" Rage swept through her, lighting her eyes with thoughts of murder. Her anger carried her in small steps around her office. Agitated pacing heightened her emotions.

"No need to plan that. I would bet my last check he is going to disappear when this is finished, anyway." Mitch pulled her back to his chest, holding her tightly. "If only I put the clues together faster, maybe—"

Regina covered his regret with her lips. Kissing him with lips and teeth, she forced her way into his mouth, using the instant heat that rose between them to cushion his blame.

His hands tightened on her arms, first to push her away and then to hold her still. He gentled the kiss, coaxing her to relax. He tasted tears before she finally gave in and stopped fighting him.

"Now all we have to do is find out if escape is possible or if we will end up dead," Regina whispered. Paranoia was part of the aggression. She wondered if it was fear and discovery or her serum taking affect. The creature inside snorted, there would be no death. The decision made final, Regina marveled at the sudden influx of confidence.

"We need a plan, that's certain," Mitch murmured into her hair. He breathed in her scent, clean and citrus sharp. His mind turned over the facility blue prints. He had a copy on the computer in his office, maybe he could find a vent line or access tunnel. He told Regina his idea. Both of them knew time was short.

"I don't know how much time is left." She held his arm as Mitch rose to leave.

"I have today or until your magic potion takes me over. Trust me. Those soldiers are battle ready every morning. Their aggression level is so far off the charts they would fight shadows in the gym. Training, muscle memory, their psi abilities keep them from killing each other or me. It won't be pretty, in any case. I'll hold out as long as possible.

We'll meet for lunch." He kissed her again.

"You gonna be okay?" He cupped the side of her face. His thumb brushed his kiss into her lower lip.

Regina took a deep breath which shuddered through her. She tried another. She nodded, her smile of reassurance weak at first. The animal inside of her shoving against her skin lent Regina her strength and confidence.

"Yeah, I can handle it. After all, it can't be worse than PMS, right?" She tried to joke. Her attempt earned her an answering smile from him before he turned and left her office.

"Right." She sighed. There was work to do, starting with a blood test to see how much of the serum was in her system. Stepping out of her office, she found the lab empty and quiet. The technician's jobs had finished as soon as injections started. With all the other reviews and retesting, they deserved a break. She set up everything to draw her blood.

Hours later Regina acknowledged the testing showed a critically elevated amount of the serum in her system. She wondered why she wasn't tearing folks apart yet. With the accumulation of the herbs in her body, her warning label should read dangerous. Yet her emotions, other than the need for forceful retribution on the liar who headed this study, seemed to be constant and, for the most part, even.

She had heard from Mitch nearly two hours ago, he found a way for them to get out of *Below*. He'd stashed the map in his room, giving her the code to get into his quarters. Unlike the labs, there was no need for a card in the military housing, everything operated on keypads.

When he had to join everyone on the lower level, she had the way out and could get away from the mad scientist, taking every note and finding that she'd started to download while she waited for the results of her blood draw. That was as safe as Mitch could make her, he'd assured her over the phone. He figured that playing it safe, taking the training and the new orders assured his way back above ground.

He would find her when he got up there. He wished he had more time with her, time he needed to tell her how he felt about her, how he wanted to be in her life. He promised himself to find her, come hell or high water.

Before their lunch date he'd received a summons to the training level. Dr. Laurel wanted him to be there to start the process of training and assimilation with the new team.

The feeling washed over him that it was too late. He was about to lose everything he'd never known he wanted.

Mitch changed in the locker room, getting ready for a beating. He was starting to acknowledge some effects of the aggression in his system. His body was burning through adrenalin like a sports drink. He wondered if the sweat on his skin looked neon in the right lighting. Bringing his mind back to his task, he walked onto the gym floor. He noted the ten men already there in much the same state he was, their eyes focused and fever bright, their bodies warmed and ready for action.

As this was the third team, he knew the steps by rote. He handed out the weapons, wrapped, cushioned with foam, banded for their ultimate safety. Sure as hell no matter how protected, these men would strike to break bones. It was now in their blood.

The dim lighting in the gym left the impression on their minds of being deep in the enemies' territory, planning an attack at dawn or dusk, when the enemies would be sleeping or letting their guard down. That's why this level was off limits until the serum did its work on the teams. The blood dark walls, lit ineffectively with low wattage bulbs, added to the shadows, to the fight reflex beginning its control of the men.

Mitch hated being here. He hated what he was doing, hated the feeling crawling under his skin. He hated knowing he was going to lose the reasoning part of his mind and become, like every team before him, an armed killing machine. He paired off everyone, making sure the cameras recorded every second in this dungeon. Let the games begin. He glanced up to the second floor observation room, giving a nod to Laurel, who stood with evil anticipation on his features, hand outstretched to change the lighting.

The lighting changed, the dimness faded into crimson, brightening the blood shade of the walls. Mitch's breathing ramped up, nostrils flaring as he struggled to contain his emotions, the urge to rend and tear filling him with incredible suddenness and strength. The ambiance of the gym added to the growing need for battle, the light absorbing through his very skin feeding the frenzy. Inside, the dragon roared his aggression, the king of this cadre, this first ever Drakken crew.

As if the roar was aloud, the battle cry echoing through the large space, every man tensed and attacked. Suddenly the sounds of battle filled the air, studded with grunts and cries as weapons struck. Blood suffused the air in mist form, the rich copper scent following as wounds opened. Every sense seemed heightened in the low light.

Mitch watched the first soldier lose conscious control of his talent, ripping his opponent open from throat to stomach with a cushioned lance. With his mind the man tore his former friend open, exposing things no one should ever see outside his body before he died.

Chapter 13

Roaring, the victor turned to hunt for his next victim. Dr. Laurel wondered when he should stop the official recording. His hand hovered above the switch. Another primordial howl had the hair rising on his arms, telling him of another death. Eleven men fought below, their actions swift, spread over the entire court, so much to watch and he wanted to miss nothing.

A safe spectator, the geneticist watched the carnage below his observation level. Cameras captured every grunt, slash, angered howl as the subjects fought to the death. He knew it would stop when he switched the lights back to bright fluorescent light. However, this team was different. As he watched them in battle, their psi talents revealed themselves. It was amazing to watch, even as he expected it to happen. The strength in their bodies and their minds combined. It was evolution at the finest, the strongest man won. He'd crossed the line he'd been hired and paid well to cross. This was the very success of his plan.

He thought of the good doctor. She'd started showing symptoms of the serum, but not the aggression. How she would react with the subdued lighting? He reached for the switch to page her to the gym. She was a female, weaker than his subjects, yet how delicious it was for him to change her chemistry to match the males in the project.

It would serve her right, without any mental abilities he'd ever discovered, she would be a true placebo to the serum's effects. He'd thought that at first he could bend her to his will, making her a partner with benefits. She'd resisted admirably, increasing his desire to have her. He would soon curb her attitude, making her his in the end. If she wanted to fight him, he'd dominate the female and show her his truth.

Turning his attention to the floor below him, he banished thoughts of Regina from his mind.

He'd so hoped this for the first of their subjects. The psi abilities uniting in a link within the soldier's natural aggression level created this unique package of ruthless killer and incredible strength.

Somehow, they'd missed the extra ingredient from the first. He'd found it when presented with the original notes he'd made long ago. Once he fixed the addition to the serum, his dream fought to life with everyone below him.

Finally a winner —this would keep him safe and sound and assure a soft and cushy retirement wherever in the world he wanted to go. As another scream split the air, he hit the switch, turning the light of day onto the carnage in the gym below him.

Mitch and the others still standing blinked in the light. As they tried to assimilate what had happened, he heard more than one of the men left standing puking in revulsion. It looked exactly like he'd have imagined berserker attack would.

Mitch counted the standing figures, some bent over, some staring about them in shock. Three men were down and, from what he glimpsed of them, they were not getting back up again. He turned and looked up to the observation booth. The rage still ran through him, even as the lighting removed the utter urge to destroy. He hoped the loss of three men was enough. His gaze met that of the mad scientist.

The light blanketed the desire to rend and tear, which likely saved Dr. Laurel's life. He saw his death in the glare Commander Bolton sent his way. The light brought them back, but only away from the violence. He evaluated the rest of the men standing. More than one of them was verging on a continuation or an escalation. He was pleased, but kept that to himself. He could not wait to forward these images to Virginia. Together, the military dollar and the discovery of a true Viking elixir for aggression had finally created the perfect fighting machine. The special bulbs reflected natural wavelengths. Dropped in a zone before first light or at twilight, the 'tween times when light curved to blood hues, the bulbs would wake the sleeping aggression. The takeover would happen quickly and violently, then when the light strengthened, the viciousness would fade, mission accomplished.

Mitch folded his arms around his stomach. If the fire would ease off he could think. It burned throughout his body, distracting his mind. Sweat dripped from him, soaking his clothes, cutting runnels down his skin dotted with blood. He fought to regain control, to be strong. He needed to be strong enough to get this mess taken care of and to handle the reports that were going topside.

He looked at his men. Two others were suffering as he was. As he watched them, one arched back in a spasm, his neck muscles locking as an anguished shriek tore from his throat. Mitch did not believe his eyes as the man melted, shifted, re-formed in a hideous blend of man and reptile.

As he watched, the shape shifted once more, becoming more reptilian, lizard-like. He felt the soldier's mind snap before anyone could help him. Crazed, he charged one of the closer men. In an instant, fast as a thought, the man retaliated against the horror charging him. A garbled roar sounded and the lizard burst, spraying all those close to him with entrails and bloody fluids.

Mitch went to his knees, watching the end of his sanity. What he witnessed could not, should not have happened. A man did not change into another creature. He looked up once more, to see the doctor leaving the observation room. He should thank the doctor for leaving the lights on. Artificial sunlight should have kept the nightmare at bay. Instead, it brought the true damages to light, damage inflicted by his teammates. The creature stared from inside, seeing the destruction and accepting it. It wanted away, needed the succor of its mate. Where was the little blue Drakken?

The sights burned into Mitch's mind, pushing him close to his limits. He felt dirty, unclean in the grisly aftermath of this trial. The rest of the men, the six of them, looked to him for guidance. He pointed them to the showers. *As if they could wash this off them.*

Hell, nothing would wash this away from them. To think they had more days of this made his stomach rebel, forcing him over, gagging on hate and rage.

Maybe it was over. Results were the good doctor's payday. Mitch wondered if he would have used deadly force on any of the men with him. He knew the others would get to wondering the same thing. The next thought sent chills skittering through his abused body. What if this was the end? How would they ever be normal now? Every one of them was a nightmarish monster and the man who changed to the lizard... Was that to be their future? To become some sort of were-creature the military would force out to fight in situations regular soldiers wouldn't be able to handle?

Was that the reason the previous men were killed? Had they changed forms in battle conditions and not recovered.

He tried to follow his team to the showers, but hard cramps shook him from head to toe. He finished his fall to his knees, going to his side and curling into a fetal position on the floor to escape the pain. He heard the door open as a clean-up team entered in environmental suits. They started cleaning the floor, taking away all evidence of what had happened there. Efficient to the last, the mad scientist kept all his bases covered. In all the tests Mitch studied, this had never happened in print. He'd been kept from watching live. Now he knew why.

A team loaded him onto a stretcher. The strange processional of stretchers, one with him tied down flat and the rest holding black body bags, entered the freight elevator and went up.

There was something wrong inside of him. He could feel it. He could not sense anything from the suited folks. In the hallway, his carriers paused beside the mad scientist himself. Laurel loomed over him, cataloguing every wince and gasp. Mitch felt his strength ebbing, the fight against his body draining him. He listened as Laurel instructed them to feed the bodies into the crematory. For the barest second Mitch thought he would welcome the certain death. Then his mind flexed and he realized he had way too much to live for now.

The dragon inside him roared, calling his Drakken brothers. No one heard but Mitch.

He sympathized with the need to regroup, but there was nothing he could do tied down as he was now. Once the straps came off, then the battle would be one on one. Laurel didn't stand a chance. He needed to pay for the criminal injustices he'd perpetrated against them, even if they had volunteered.

Mitch fought for clarity, tried to argue with the doctor, who smiled hatefully into his face. Mitch fought the paralysis that claimed his limbs. The pain slipping away in waves.

"You don't seem to understand. You are the only obstacle to this whole venture. You interfered with Regina. You found secrets better left secret and shared them. Your usefulness has come and gone. When you vanish I will be here to bend Regina to my will. With her abilities she should be tractable. I will enjoy handling her, helping her over your loss. What a pity, your loss." Stepping back, he waved them away.

Mitch watched the lights pass as he rolled down the hall, those hate-filled words echoing in his head.

He called Regina with all the focus he could from the fire engulfing him internally. He knew convulsions and death had to follow this fever. His body was literally burning up from the inside. He prepared himself to die. Before they cleared the biology department Regina appeared at his side. He looked at her. Her eyes were wide and tear-filled, searching him from head to toe. He knew she asked for details, but he could not hear her voice with his ears.

He reached for her hand. He thought he reached for it. Regina took his hand in hers. She was so cool. Her touch a balm against the heat eating him alive. He tried to let her know what happened in the gym, feeding her his memory. Her hand tightened on his, but somehow she thought he was already dead.

He kept talking to her, his head ringing with his thoughts. He assured her he would get back to her. Her greatest fear realized, she believed she was looking at her own death. He could hear her thoughts clearly, why couldn't she hear his? Staring into his eyes, she knew her turn was coming. Her head jerked up, but he couldn't see what happened. Then Laurel entered his frozen line of sight.

Mitch watched impotently as the mad scientist lied to Regina. He watched her believe the lies. She looked back at him, her eyes wild with fear. She was alone, surrounded by liars, people she couldn't trust. What was worse, he could not protect her. He tried to tell her what he knew, but he was fading, thoughts tumbling and burning in the crucible of heat and pain, vaporizing against his will. He was dead to her.

Eyes fixed open, he watched her shrug off Laurel's sympathetic advances. His focus shifted to Regina, her bright eyes, her flaming hair, her brilliant mind, her certain death. Fire blazed in her eyes as she demanded answers, solutions. He'd failed. The shadows closed, leaving the vivid flicker of her etched in his mind.

The heat when they opened the furnace brought him to awareness. His body welcomed the flare of the extreme. The mere hundred ten degrees of his body was cool compared to the fifteen hundred degrees of the oven. Designed to bake him to ashes and bone bits, it would destroy every bit of evidence of the experiments done on the volunteers. That would be the end, no family to ever come forward and ask questions of the great volunteers who would likely follow.

They rolled him onto the platform and pushed it into the oven without ceremony. There the heat engulfed him, warming places inside that started to chill.

That stubborn spark in his brain tripped along on some endorphin high. It keened for the flames, the heat surrounding his body. The door closed, the air became thin and difficult to breathe. The restraints about his arms and legs fell away with wet sizzles and he sat up on the table. He should be dead, his body soaked in the flames, the core of him matching the fevered heat of his skin. His strength returned, he realized he was strong enough to get out of here. Before he could move further, that voice of caution spoke, a murmur of prudence, watchfulness.

He relaxed, allowing the heat to wash him clean. His muscles spasmed and tensed, his spine arched, his breathing deepened, finally gathering enough oxygen to fill his lungs. Time passed as his body trembled and relaxed in turns. He found a total release of tension and fell asleep. *So this is death.* A dark quiet, a brain-dead kind of slumber from which he did not expect to wake.

Cool air jarred him to consciousness. He heard a voice urgently calling on a radio. The squawk hurt his ears. Shaking the noise from his head, Mitch sat up on the table. Ashes sifted to the floor at his movement.

He listened to that frantic voice for another moment, coming fully awake and aware. He was outside the crematory with one male in the same room. The radio whistled against his eardrums, beating at his sensitive hearing. He moved in reaction. Taking the radio in hand, he twisted until plastic fell between his crushing fingers, permanently stopping the noise.

The mental vibrations he received from the other male made him wary. Before the weapon cleared the holster, Mitch's animal brain took over and he killed the threat. Taking a moment, he put on scrubs he found. He was thankful the shoes he found were usable, because the floor was damn cold. His feet started to warm up. He hated cold feet.

Following survival instincts and memories of the facility, he made his way topside. A small voice reminded him that Regina was still a prisoner, but the animal part of him, the Drakken claiming him, was stronger now, demanding he follow instinct, forced him away from the base and farther from her. Survival was the urgent demand, an order he could not ignore.

He would return, he promised, when he could control himself. He did not want to go through life a mindless killing machine. That very fear beat against his soul as memories returned in full color and high def sound.

He believed the mad scientist wanted Regina alive and unharmed, so she would be safer here. He also knew her strength, maybe better than she did herself. She was strong enough to keep it together until he could return. He made himself believe that, forcing his body into tight spaces and dark places, until he made it to the desert surrounding the facility.

He holed up in a pocket of shade at the base of a sun-drenched butte. Splitting cactus for water, he shrugged off the sweat soaked scrub top and rested. He watched the sun cross the sky and the shadows growing around him. Soon he would be able to move again. All day listening for air support proved the R&D facility did not have the budget for that kind of protection. Funds allocated to security were probably small to non-existent. So much the better for him.

He waited until twilight, when the day was gone but the night not fully born. He sighed and stood to start moving. Time to go. Where, he didn't know. Now AWOL from the military he realized he could face severe penalties, up to execution. Nothing different there from the twenty-four of his men fucked by this experiment, the dead and wounded in mind and body were expendable. He shook his head and moved out of the shade to start away from the base. It was then the change hit him.

Mitch fell. His legs trembled beyond his control. He face planted into the sand, the lingering heated embrace cushioning his body. He rolled so he could breathe, but the muscle contractions forcing him into weird contortions had his breathing coming in short pants. He moaned, and then roared as his bones liquefied, changing shape.

Indescribable pain tore his muscles from his ligaments and then, for good measure, split his bones. His heart raced then burst. It took up a double beat, trying to process the flood of adrenalin flowing through him from the agony. The memory of the soldier who went reptile replayed in a sickening reel. Mitch rolled to his side, dry heaves barely noticeable in the havoc already possessing him.

Chapter 14

When he could breathe again he was on his knees, the glow of the moon on his head and bare back. The weight of the light blanketed him, and for a moment he wondered if he'd be able to stand. He opened his eyes, blinking in the brightness. A muted brightness, his eyesight was different, colors and brighter shades dulled. The world lit around him as with infrared lenses.

He looked to his body. He blinked. He raised both hands closer to his eyes. Yep, they were his. These clawed, scaled talons were his hands. His thighs were also covered in scales, his stomach ridged in two or three six packs now as he gazed along the lengthened torso. Those muscles of his stomach sported the same rich red scales. He clamped his jaw, keeping the strangled noise of madness trapped in his throat.

He'd been transformed from human to some creature out of a twisted imagination. Unable to see the whole of his body, he tried to stand, craning his head around.

His arms pushed him upright. But when he looked at his shadow another surprise awaited him. In the shadow of the rising moon, he lifted an arm to reach around to touch a wing. Echoes of madness struck him, memories crowding in and overriding sane thought. He'd changed, much like the others in the test, he was reptilian. His mind shied from any thought of dragons, wanting to pounce on the word as his new identity.

Moving helped and Mitch wandered around the desert in shock for the night, trying to disbelieve his new reality. How would he change back? Was the moon to blame? He certainly wasn't a were-wolf, so did that make him a were-dragon? The word Drakken surfaced and as his mind slowly returned to normal thought patterns, the definition filled in. It was the Swedish word for dragon, an old tongue for an extinct creature. He liked it better than dragon, but that might have been because the very thought of being a dragon beckoned madness too close.

When stray thoughts of sanity broke into his mind, he cursed the military, the doctor, the woman he fell in love with. If not for her, he'd never have been deployed to this project. He would not have his better nature, the one that insisted he protect those who couldn't protect themselves, involved in this madness of a super soldier. He would be a naval commander working through this enlistment, dreaming of a retirement without nightmares.

She'd caused this change in him, fed the mania he tried to keep locked away. She became the focus of his hatred, the love he had had for her as deep now as the hatred that ruled him. That terribly fine line crossed in the madness of his rebirth. The struggle inside his mind and soul fed off an animal nature he'd never acknowledged. The creature he'd become lived with another idea of the woman in question.

Restless, the Drakken tried to convince him to go back, to return to the very dungeon of its birth to find her. Mitch fought the instinct, his footsteps dogging the desert as the internal war waged between man and animal. The Drakken wanted his mate. Mitch scoffed, railing against the need rising. Voice filling the bright darkness, he argued and stumbled under the weight of the monster he'd become.

In time, when he'd walked the desert in the cold night, his body went through another transition, back to the human one. Before dawn the smell of food led him to a desert commune in the middle of nowhere. Fed and given a place to rest, he thanked the members for the hospitality. They were simple folks who wanted to live their own lives.

He lived with them a couple of weeks, gradually learning the rhythm of their life, living in fear of the Drakken. No one asked for his history and he gradually relaxed into a new way of living, letting the day take care of needs, and keeping the night free of nightmares. Accepted at face value, he settled into existence with them.

One night almost two weeks since his escape, he came across the oldest man in the commune. A pocket Buddha, Chin Yeo spent time with Mitch that night. It seemed to Mitch as if the little monk knew somehow of his other self. Talking in broken English, Chin Yeo told Mitch his history. A martial arts expert and wise man, he came to America for the freedom to live his last days.

His family gone from him, he had given all to the country of his birth. Now the country had no use for him, so he left. To be free in

America, that was a dream, his dream. He was simple, as were the folks he eventually found. They were a match. When he died they would take care of his body, sending him back to his spiritual ancestors.

Mitch found the little man good for his soul, a buffer for the anger and hate that ate at him daily, hourly, trying to consume every second of his existence.

Chin Yeo began teaching Mitch, helping Mitch step away from those tangled emotions. Allowing the xuésheng to get beyond the tragedy Chin Yeo sensed in Mitch became his work. Mitch regained his sense of self while learning the ways of the Drakken or dragon as Chin Yeo kept calling the force inside Mitch.

Chin Yeo worked with Mitch and showed no fear of the appearance of Mitch's dragon, wings and all. Together they explored the body of the beast, and worked on learning the limits of this form. Mitch managed to grow emotional scar tissue over his heart. He remembered the emerald ring he'd bought to give Regina, a promise to her that they would be together, a plea that she wait for him, the life lost as he shifted forms and learned to accept. Would it stay stashed in his quarts forever?

He spent countless hours in the desert with the wizened Chinese teacher. They repeated the same lessons. The little lǎoshī never seemed surprised by his transformation from man to Drakken. He even managed to help Mitch trigger the full red dragon. That beast was twenty-seven feet from head to tail, a forgotten nightmare returned to life.

Shaking the rocks and dust from the avalanche off his body, Mitch coughed to clear his lungs, nearly setting Chin Yeo on fire. Jumping behind another fall of rocks saved Chin Yeo's life.

"You are good, Red?"

"I'm okay. I didn't singe you, did I?"

Chin Yeo moved from his fire block. "I am okay, Red. You did not expect to have that." Hands clasped behind his back, he stood before the great dragon. Mitch shook his head. Another small wisp of steam seeped from the side of his mouth.

"It is good. You are learning."

Mitch growled, the sound hollow as it traveled the length of his sinuous neck. *"All I do is learn."* It was a common complaint. Yet his memory was strong of his rebirth and he understood there was to be a learning curve. At least he wasn't in this alone. Chin Yeo kept him from self-destructing. He was grateful, yes, but impatience chaffed as the feeling that time was running out for him nagged.

"It is what must happen for you to survive. You do not belong here. There is a life waiting for you, people looking for you." He stepped close to the dragon and reached out to touch the scaled leg closest to him.

"Your heart does not beat with strength. You are missing the key to contentment."

Mitch stepped back. He was better, but not ready to explore any of his past.

Letting the moment pass, Chin Yeo stepped back, then climbed to be closer to the dragon's eye line. "Time to fly."

Oceans of blood, sweat, and tears later Mitch took to the skies. His gas bladders were full, assisting in the lift of his heavy body. He swept his wings and allowed himself to take flight.

Alone for the first time, he soared over the desert, far away from civilization. Freedom eased the weight on his heart. He took joy in the airborne speed he achieved. The aerial play tired him, yet he knew there would be more practice.

He stumbled to a landing close to Chin Yeo. The little monk rested his hand against the great beating heart. The dragon let go the form and the man fell exhausted to his knees. They stayed away from the commune that night and other nights after the big transformation. Chin Yeo fashioned a harness, which allowed him to ride the great red body into the sky.

Mitch followed the taps on his neck and wings, learning the aerodynamics of this form, so different from the smaller dragon, more suited to gliding.

The only unfortunate consequence of his changing forms was his roaring need for sex. Neither of them were doctors, so they only had theories to work with. They agreed it stemmed from the primitive brain. The animal mind focused on food, rest and sex. Driven to mate, his instinct to procreate forced Mitch's body into sexual over-drive. When he came back as a man, the chemical cocktail drenched his system. The urge to fuck was so great he forced his painfully aroused body to the deep pool in a claimed cave and brought his body to orgasm repeatedly until his cock finally stopped hardening.

Chin Yeo disappeared after Drakken changed to man, leaving

Mitch time and privacy to take care of his needs.

When all Mitch wanted to do was fall into exhausted slumber, Chin Yeo forced him to eat and then to exercise, working the stiffness from every muscle and regaining the mental balance the commander needed.

This torture became life as Mitch knew it. He did not have to think. He lived to act and react. Chin Yeo worked on his spirituality as well as his body. Hours of meditation, guided by the monk or working alone, increased his mental shields and his mental strengths. He discovered the rest of the mixed bag of psi talents he possessed. Becoming familiar with the way they worked, he tested his telekinesis, strengthened his telepathy, since that was the only way the dragon could communicate with Chin Yeo.

Chin Yeo worked his body, using an ancient form predating biofeedback. He taught Mitch how to regulate his breathing, his heartbeat. Chin Yeo helped him to call the dragon without pain, from one form or the other.

Mitch's sex drive became manageable. He began to hold his body in full arousal until after a meal, and then managed to stretch it to almost two hours before he became a slave to his need.

The desert life was not without rewards. Chin Yeo brought him willing women who wanted to be with him from the commune. He enjoyed the encounters. The female body was his endless source of delight. He made sure to give more than he ever received, leaving his partners sated and exhausted.

If thoughts of riotous red curls intruded, he banished them like a bad dream. If he hungered for plump, full breasts and creamy honey that haunted his taste buds, the taste an unmatched memory in his head, those thoughts he bound into a box, locked with his broken heart. The pain there became anger, the anger acceptance, the acceptance in time resembled cold hate and the need for revenge.

Mitch wondered when his mind and heart were still as the desert night, if the military *cleansed* the base where his alter ego was born. That would mean all life forms still *Below* were exterminated, the base a buried pile of misguided delusions.

The voice of his heart whispered to him that she was not to blame. The voice asked him what hell she went through. The voice asked him when he would return for her. He locked the voice into the box, listening to it no more.

That was behind him now. The military considered him dead. That life died in the furnace that gave birth to the internal animal that guided him from insanity to an accord. The Drakken had his agenda. He would go back for his mate, for his struggling brothers in arms, for revenge. That string of thought grew stronger as it moved through the Drakken's mind, becoming a chain that dragged on his heart, tangled his soul, searched for his mate.

There was no time in the desert, day followed night-followed day. His body hardened to a weapon. He began to long for the regiment of duty and the chaotic press of life. Chin Yeo passed one night, peaceful in death as in life. Mitch lit the pyre, taking to the air to mourn the monk in the form he'd worked so diligently to master.

Chapter 15

As though the little master's death was a herald, it marked time for Mitch to leave the desert. He worked his way east, never staying in one place for any length of time, never taking the time to contact his family. It didn't take him long. The weather cooled as he passed the miles. There were times he used the fake ID he'd procured when he couldn't get mercenary jobs. Most of his bosses didn't check that closely into the legalities. Some search and rescue and a few jobs to recover items misplaced put money in his pockets. Those he didn't look into closely. He took his pay in cash, his wounds in stride and kept his alter ego hidden.

He missed the big fire Drakken. The freedom and inherent power was such a part of him in the desert. It had been out once on his journey back to life.

Tonight, on foreign soil, his talents assuring him a princely sum to end a string of weapons merchants, he allowed the Drakken his freedom. Almost ten months had passed since he'd pointed himself east and let his feet carry him to the Atlantic Ocean.

Acknowledging his sexual relief would be alone, he transformed. Chin Yeo had been dead those months, yet the little monk's spirit seemed to join him on this flight.

He took to the black night, kissed in darkness by a new moon. He cast no reflections, starlight the only glow against his red scales. He stretched his body, covering miles in the night sky. The pumping of his great wings was silent in the wash of air, no louder than the greatest owl. His heart beat with the now familiar double pulse in his chest. After eating a mountain goat for dinner, he washed it down with cold water from a mountain stream. It was time to return. He had a timetable he needed to follow. These stolen moments were short and sweet.

He headed out of the snow-covered peaks, back toward the jungle and his duties. Returning to the clearing where he stashed his clothes and pack, he slipped deeper into the jungle before giving into his body's demands. His hand grasped his straining cock, that firm touch triggered the first eruption. He sagged against a tree trunk, settling to his knees in the forest loam.

Pumping his fist along his length, his mind wished for the soft tugging of lips, the snap and flicker of an interested tongue. Again, he shot a milky load into the air, coating his hand for more strokes. His head rested against the smooth bark of the tree as his body pushed higher, muscles trembling in orgasm. He moaned a mere breath of sound. His other hand reached below his straining cock to grasp his balls. He pulled and rolled them around, using the sensations to coax another ejaculation from his throbbing cock. Finally slowing his actions, he took control back.

Tucking his still hard cock back into his pants, the lingering sensations made him shiver. The effort of pounding between a willing woman's thighs beat the rough stroking of his hand any day. He missed a woman, his woman, his mate. The dragon inside him keened, but Mitch ignored the mournful sound. He had a duty to fulfill.

He headed toward the pick-up point. The night leached back toward day before he reached the area. He set the beacon and then faded into the jungle. Mitch settled in the coming dawn, unmoving, becoming part of the flora and fauna around him. He remained so quiet and still in body and mind the night's predators walked past his hiding place. He watched the slow slink of a cloud leopard, the misty gray coat blending in the coming light.

He watched as the cloud leopard's larger cousin stalked past going the other way. The leopard froze within touching distance and Mitch told himself later that he should have paid more attention to his fellow animals. When the leopard faded into the brush like shadow, it was way too late for Mitch. He sighed when the barrel of the rifle settled in the neckline of his flak-vest.

"Get up slowly, you're coming with us." The voice was female, the accent deep south, and the tone dead serious. He looked across the clearing, watching camouflaged soldiers come out of the jungle. It looked like the latest payday would be half-short, no way could he collect the last of it now. The day of reckoning was here.

"Commander Mitchell Bolton, I presume." The leader walked over to him. The beam of his flashlight struck Mitch in the face, not quite blinding him but close. The enhanced senses rose, keeping his sight keen.

"Do I get a prize if I'm the one?"

"No one said anything about a sense of humor. We were warned about your aggressive tendencies." The figure walked completely around Mitch. Mitch hadn't moved a muscle since the chill of steel touched his neck. He didn't move now, listening as the beaten air forced against his eardrums foretold of the chopper closing in on their location. The bird would have alerted the recon team he originally waited for. They'd be a country away by now.

"You don't seem to be a threat, but please don't take it wrong if we do not take any chances." He stopped in front of Mitch. "We're here to take you home, Commander, seems like you have been MIA for some time."

The rifle prodded him in the back as the helicopter settled down in the clearing. The swift spin of the rotors barely cleared the tangle of jungle vines ringing the perimeter. He joined the team loading into the bay. Mitch was resolute about going home. If they were looking for a deserter, he guessed they would have shot him and left him to rot. With the MIA comment, Mitch had the uneasy feeling he was about to be called back into official duty. He settled down for the ride. Might as well, it was going to be a long trip back to the states.

His mind could not turn it loose, though. He kept his own council, waiting to see if anyone would drop any other comments. The best he could put together, the facility probably reported his AWOL status. Assuming they did so, the military knew his condition, leaving him a "loose cannon" possibly dangerous if the information gathered on the experiment had made it to the right connections.

He was sure the mad scientist gave the government most of his findings. Like any capitalist, he'd kept the best to himself. Insurance, of a sort, for his future survival and eventual retirement.

Lieutenant Jones escorted Mitch into barracks, leaving him in a gilded cage. Mitch did not for a minute think he was free to explore. He settled down on the bunk. His backpack already searched, he used it as a backrest. He didn't carry a weapon, didn't need one. The 9mm Ruger SR9 they'd removed from his backpack was a last tie to the life he'd left behind. All he'd packed was a change of clothes, a small wrap holding a couple of things he kept from Chin Yeo, and some protein bars. His money, banked electronically, waited for him online or through the card he carried in the lining of his pack, not easy to find.

Mitch cooled his heels, still and quiet. He was wondering if breakfast came with the room when the door opened and he received the answer. Sure enough, the tour led him to a mess hall. He got in line with his escort, taking a little of everything. He stopped to look around the mess, waiting for his escort. He saw Lieutenant Jones waving him to his table. He nodded and started forward.

"Sorry about the accommodations, Commander. You know we are still filling in the official channels about your successful rescue." Jones spoke around his own breakfast.

"Rescue, that's what you call it now? No problem. Since you 'rescued' me, when am I to expect a trip home?" Mitch settled across from Jones, tucking into his breakfast.

"As I understand it, you were thought to be exposed to a contagion." Jones looked him over. "It doesn't seem to have done you any harm. We received intelligence on you in this area fourteen hours ago. Evidently, the hunt-you-down order is nearly six months old. We happened to get the dog-catching privilege." Jones pushed his tray away. Taking his coffee cup in both hands, he sipped and watched Mitch. "No offense."

"Is that all you know about the contagion?" Mitch could not stop the question, knowing he probably would not get an answer.

"No, the research and development facility was shut down, the experiments were not coming out as theorized. Like a lot of things we try, it was a bust." A careless shrug accompanied the dismissal.

Mitch remembered the smell of the gym after the first encounter of his team. He pushed his tray away. If Jones only knew...

"The doctor in charge, Emerson Laurel?" Mitch tuned into the man's thoughts, knowing he wouldn't say how much he really knew.

"He moved his research into new digs, private, somewhere on the east coast, I believe." Jones sipped his coffee. The eyes told him Bolton had seen a lot. He did not know if it was due to the lab or the way the man had been living, so far off the radar. He caught glimpses of hell, shadows that told him this sailor had seen too much. Whatever battle Bolton endured, it burned most of the humanity from him. No matter how bad they wanted his return, this was a husk of the person they remembered as Bolton. He'd become an unstable bomb returning to an alien environment.

Jones was past retirement age, but having lost all his family, he stayed in the service. He studied Bolton, foreign to a man who clung to duty, this man lived without rules and guides. Jones wondered how Bolton lived with the dichotomy. A decorated officer, handpicked for missions few others would accept, he'd volunteered to live underground in a secret facility for who knew what kind of experimentation.

A shell of the former military commander, Bolton ate with little attention to the food he shoveled into his mouth, arm curled around the tray as if worried someone would take it away. Jones leaned back, thinking of all the information missing in this man's dossier. Lean and rangy, he looked younger than the age on the page. Hair slicked back from his face, the leather tie keeping it under control, he hadn't seen a barber in a year or more.

He'd been tagged with a nickname by the underground he'd moved through in true survival mode. Desert Dragon fit him in some way, the way Bolton studied his surroundings and peeled back the flesh and bone of the person he chose to study, as he studied Jones now.

"I believe you will be stopping by there on your way back." Jones let him have that piece of information. He watched Bolton as he slipped into complete inhuman stillness. Things stirred through his expression, things Jones had better sense than to inquire about. He stood to get more coffee.

"When you're ready, I'll have them escort you back to shower and rest. I do not expect your transfer flight to connect until this afternoon." Jones turned to walk away. Looking back, he stopped.

"I don't suppose you have a passport?"

Mitch looked back at him, blinked, didn't move a muscle.

"And the military ID?"

The blank gaze, giving nothing away, told him everything he needed to know. Jones shook his head. "Get cleaned up and I'll have someone get you proper paperwork to get you back stateside." He looked at Mitch with a resigned smile. "Legally."

Mitch watched him walk away. Legal, yeah, the biggest joke. What had been legal about murdering those men? And the rest of the team left over in the carnage? What about Regina? What was her fate at the hands of that power/money hungry fiend using her in her own experiment?

The whole of the past attempted to break from the prison in his mind. Barely healed wounds throbbed in need of closure. He had no answers, but he knew as surely as the sun rose today he was to be in the thick of things in no time. Patience, he cautioned as he caught the eye of his guard. Jones finished speaking with him, nodded in Mitch's direction and left the mess hall. The guard stepped over to Mitch.

"Ready to go, sir?" If he hadn't finished eating, the answer would have been the same. Better to face the future quickly if they were going to present it to him like a gift.

"Yes." Mitch stood. Pulling the backpack over his shoulder, he followed his escort to better quarters with a bath. He quickly showered, not wanting to be out of sight of his bag long. The only locks were outside the door. He wrapped a towel around his hips, enjoying the feeling of being clean. His last shower had been nine days ago. He'd used the muddy waters of rivers and creeks after setting foot in this country.

Stepping out of the bath, he noted a set of BDUs on the bed, with all rank insignia. Piled beside them was another set, underwear in boxer and brief, socks, new boots, and toiletries, some he had forgotten how to use.

He went back into the bathroom and shaved without too many nicks. He brushed his teeth, but the mint flavor of the paste was too strong and he ended up using the brush after spitting out the sweet goo. Finishing the finer touches, he put the uniform on. Good fit. Confirming that he was under surveillance, as soon as he double knotted his boots the door opened.

"If you would please follow me, Commander?" The corporal stepped into the corridor. "You may leave your things here, you will be returning to this room." Mitch hesitated, yet gleaned nothing from the steady gaze of the corporal. Mitch relented and left the bag and other things in an artless, yet intricate pattern on the bed. If anyone touched it, he would know. *Time to smile for the camera.*

Two days later, he was stateside and legal. This time he sensed Regina in the edge of his consciousness. There was a growing need to see her, hold her. It was a feeling he was getting used to, the pressure against his talent from the brief closeness he'd felt with her. The Drakken grew more insistent, scraping against his tentative hold.

He ground his teeth through an honorable discharge, a debrief during which he claimed to have amnesia. He prayed hourly that none of this information would reach Laurel and chaffed every second he was required to stay in the smothering grasp of the military.

His last meeting with Greg found him sharing things in confidence, things only family should know, things he'd artfully denied to the psychologist assigned to him. Over-scheduled and underappreciated, the doctor was doing his best. Mitch gave him the answers he expected and wanted to hear. He dismissed Mitch with flying colors, sanity intact on the paperwork.

"It was a risk sending you into the system. It seems to have paid off. Six months AWOL and you look like you did two years ago when you accepted the orders to enter the trials."

"You do know every soldier was killed."

"I do. It was unfortunate and unexpected."

"Bull shit, Greg. You were in on this from the start. That's how you pulled the strings to get me inside."

His cousin stared at him through whisky goggles. Greg shook his head, dropping his gaze. "I was involved, not from the outset, but shortly thereafter. I wanted those soldiers to survive and prove the value."

"Making money not in your long range plans?"

"It wasn't like that." Greg took to his feet, pacing the length of his living room. One wall opened to the city lights, a nice view. Being a General had its perks, it seemed. They were sitting in the dark, Greg a shadow moving slowly, trailing a scent of the bourbon he sipped.

"Then try to explain it. I was there. I found out the hard way what was happening."

"It was supposed to be exactly what it was presented to be."

"Nothing was as it was presented. Those men tore each other apart. I don't know what the difference was between the first two trials and ours, but there was a great divide. I trained with all three teams before the trials. My team, the last one to face the music, went psychotic in minutes." Mitch hesitated, but the whisky was stronger. "Something happened to me down there, Greg. Something—" He shook his head as Greg stopped at the window, turning to face him across the dark room.

"What was it?" There was no surprise in his voice, yet dread colored the edges of every softly spoken word.

"There were changes to some of the men, to me."

"What kind of changes?" Hushed, tense, Greg remained

unmoving in the wash of light coming into the room from behind him.

"They were reptilian, huge in stature, vicious fighters." Mitch swallowed bile, leaning forward to put his drink on the table. If he held it much longer he'd end up crushing the fragile glass. "We fought with no thought of mercy in our heads." Mitch curled his arms around his stomach. "I was killed."

Chapter 16

Greg's glass hit the tile floor, the shattering noise loud between them.

"How do you know?" He took a step forward, and then he thought better and straightened. A hoarse grunt betrayed his interest.

"I woke up in a cremation oven. The flames were fully engaged."

"How is it that you're here now?" Greg moved across the room, looking closely at Mitch as he took a seat on the coffee table. The two men now sat knee to knee.

"I somehow used the heat to revive." He glanced up at Greg, sitting military straight in front of him. "It changed something in me. I have another form, like a were-creature."

Just like that, Greg threw back his head and laughed. The tension broke, but Mitch didn't join in the mirth.

"You had me going there, cuz. I was with you and then, gods' balls. You are funny."

"Get out of the way." Mitch's command actually moved Greg off the table. He pushed past his cousin, finding space and turning to look at Greg. Mitch took a deep breath. In an instant, he'd changed forms to the smaller of the two Drakken.

"This is not a joke."

Greg heard the words in his mind. Surely that long muzzle couldn't form them. His father had been right. Their genetic makeup was geared toward a shifting of species. Fascinated, he stepped closer, halting when the seven-foot creature hissed.

"What, how did you know?"

"There wasn't a knowing." Mitch let the hold go and his body settled back to human. Unfortunately, his clothes didn't make it. In minutes, Greg had another change in hand.

"Thanks." Mitch dressed while Greg cleaned up the broken glass and turned on a light. Not that it helped clear any of the confusion. Seated again with a fresh drink, Mitch continued.

"There was carnage around me and a pain inside that was ripping me open. A medical team appeared, rolling me onto a stretcher. They took me past Laurel, the gloating, lying bastard. He sent me to the crematory for disposal with three of the others." He clasped his hands between his knees, leaned forward on his elbows.

"I was loaded into the oven at close to fifteen hundred degrees. I guess I passed out. I woke up when they pulled me from the oven, causing panic in one of the guards on Laurel's team. I tore up the radio and killed him before making my way topside and escaping."

"Where did you go all this time?" They talked until the sun rose, the golden light erasing the shadows of the night, only to highlight the lack of sleep on both men's faces. It was a night of discovery, of storytelling of the first order. While Mitch had a greater understanding of his condition, Greg found himself envious of his cousin's ability to transform into another creature.

Time sped up for Mitch after the weekend he spent with Greg. In a week he was inducted into service under the all-reaching umbrella of Homeland Security, something he'd embraced. It came after a rushed honorable discharge, orchestrated by Greg Dolca and placed in his hands with more medals than he could hold. His uniform looked like a paint ball nightmare.

Nothing ever surfaced to him about the lab and he never brought it up. It haunted his days and woke him with nightmares, the echo of Regina's tears dragging him from restless slumber. He fought to put it away, deeply hidden inside. Yet the mention from Jones that he would be going back there had blasted the locks Mitch devised to keep the memories at bay. He turned to his new responsibilities with intense focus, keeping the secret of his dragon.

The new job represented a way to right more wrongs. He worked operations not so very different from those he'd chosen as a mercenary. Along with the new title, he had to assemble a team to work with, people already vetted through the selection process. Mitch had taken his time, never hesitating to use Greg and his contacts for more information on any given candidate.

He'd chosen his team well. A ragged bunch of ex military and mercenaries, he'd forged them into a solid, dependable and multi-talented team. Wild cards, they followed their own pursuits until called up.

Three men and a woman, they were close mouthed and experts at what they knew. Their psi talents were null. He'd checked that out as he assembled the team. He wasn't exactly the most sane at times, and he damn sure didn't want a team member in his head, ever.

The notable exception was Benjamin Dughan. They needed a medic, something Mitch sorely missed during his days as a gun for hire. Ben fit the job. But he had other talents that made his psi scores immeasurable by any tests Mitch found. His brain functioned differently than any other, including Mitch's.

On that thought, Mitch found more deviations existed in his brain now. He wondered if the cause was due to Chin Yeo's influences, the dragon's, or his life of day-to-day existence. No matter, he had enough to get the job done, and he felt safe and could keep his team safe because of the psi nulls. He refused to allow thoughts of the lab or the desert to intrude. That battle he was slowly winning.

Life began to settle. He stopped jumping at noises and he bought a hunting cabin deep in the Smoky Mountains, surrounded by one hundred sixty three acres of nothing but thick timber. Far enough away from the tourist traps, he never heard the helicopter tours over his land. The cabin kept the rain and snow off him until he'd permanently moved in.

Once he took full ownership of the rundown hunting lodge, he made changes. He reinforced the floors in the loft and the main floor, updated the plumbing and electrical and put in heat and air. He reinforced the walls from the inside. Nothing less than a tank or armor-piercing round above fifty calibers would come through the old logs. The inside was fire proofed as much as possible, and he'd had Jake up twice to create and install a security system the government would envy.

The team member lived for a good challenge.

He wasn't much of a decorator, but now he could address creature comforts. He'd built a huge bed, enough room for three to sprawl. He chose colors that in retrospect reminded him of the dry heat and the chilling cold nights of the desert. He painted them anyway, as if needing the comfort of knowing it wasn't that far away.

The fireplace had a huge, thick rug before it. He knew she'd like it. And the kitchen he outfitted for her to cook, with enough room for them to work together. All this he did without any acknowledgement of building this nest for the woman he wouldn't remember and couldn't forget.

Here the Drakkens could be free and big brother would not know. In the time he spent playing mercenary, he'd learned a few things. He kept in good practice. He purchased the place through fifteen buyers, no name on the deed. He switched cars and bikes between the city and the mountains, so no trackers followed him beyond the first one or two vehicle switches. A corporation paid all the bills and renovation costs and he took all the food he would need when he went up. There was no road in or out. The dragon-kin packed all the food into the property as needed.

Returning one evening from a walk in the misty forest, he opened the door to find a message on his laptop. He watched the light for a moment. The ruddy glow flashed in the dusky shadows of twilight. Memories fought to surface, another time, and another light releasing the hold he kept on them.

Mitch had two more days leave. They knew that. He closed the door and toed off his shoes. The damp made his feet cold. He started a fire and made something to eat before he gave in to the summons. Whatever was calling him off his leave wasn't going to be good.

Placing his feet inches from the flames, he opened the email. He read it through, letting the words flow over him, but they didn't stick. He watched the flames over the top of the folded laptop for a moment, and then he read it again. He studied each word of the missive. Every nuance of the message he absorbed. He finally closed the window and opened the dossiers attached.

Mitch studied the file photos that did her no justice. In life her hair was vibrant, her blue eyes shifted shades with her moods. Her fair complexion glowed with creamy color. He wondered when these were taken. She looked flat, her eyes gray, again she wore matching shadows beneath them. She'd lost weight. He picked at her critically. He'd written her out of his heart, trying to live a half existence without her.

As luck would have it, she was the next mission.

No longer top-secret, the facility that bred his Drakken had fallen under control by an unknown party. The research, most of it, went to points unknown with Dr. Laurel, but the developmental procedures remained, under the alleged direction of Laurel's assistant, Dr. Regina Gardner.

Dr. Laurel's last official input was that the final team didn't take the treatments well, some not reacting at all, so the project was shelved, in light of better opportunities.

For the last twelve months Dr. Gardner was nominally in charge of the underground research and development facility. Retained to find out what went wrong with the project, she and those *Below* with her were now at risk.

In a way he was happy. The facility hadn't been destroyed in the aftermath of his creation and escape. In another, he hated the need and the dumb luck that were taking him back to the place of his hell-spawned birth. For now he ignored the rush of feelings beginning to waken, memories surfacing past his careful shields. He turned back to the information collected for the mission ahead for his team.

The facility had dropped off line with all communication feeds a week ago. Two days after the failure to respond to a query, the team members that went in for recovery were all deceased. Their bodies were set out in the desert, captured by satellite imaging. They hadn't been eaten or transformed,. Their bodies were clearly marked by bullet wounds and blood stains.

Mitch figured only he would think of animal attack. At least his men left from the last team hadn't remained in animal form and were not eating each other *Below*.

The picture wasn't any prettier from what he gleaned from the information in the files, sketchy as it was. The team he'd left still resided there, under the direction of Dr. Gardner, as a continuation of the experiments.

Anger surged past the careful hold he kept of his emotions. It served no purpose. Yet this was too close to his core fury, the woman, the failure, the desertion.

The son of a bitch left her to deal with the chaos that reigned. Infected, she was left to handle the team's aggression, locked *Below* with no way out. A shudder wracked him. More of his emotions sprang free of the box he kept locked. Both Drakken forms fought for freedom, their voices roaring in aggression and power.

His woman or she once was, fought daily for the last year. No wonder she looked so haggard in her picture. He cautioned himself against caring, trying to corral his thoughts of Regina and get every one of them locked securely away again. Wasn't going to happen. The Drakkens made that perfectly clear. He'd been forced to leave her. They wanted her back.

He got to his feet, pacing to control the urge to shift forms and take to the skies, winging his way west. The dragons fought his hold on them, together nearly overpowering the discipline he'd worked so diligently to strengthen against his animal nature.

He was as much to blame as Laurel. He'd had a choice when he got free of the furnace. He could have gone back or gotten out. He could have been there to help her put the pieces back together, worked with them all to achieve some functioning way of accepting and living through the nightmare that had gripped him on that gymnasium floor. The insanity was the first step, and then together as the team he was so proud of, they could have adapted and learned. They'd be the Drakken Brotherhood, an incredible team of creatures, maybe not exactly like Mitch, but bound together with the dark history of their birth.

Battered and damaged, he'd first sought refuge to regroup. Some would consider his decisions a coward's way out. He'd challenge everyone to survive what he'd managed to live through and still be sane. Human, he'd had to step away or become a mindless being.

He stopped that line of thought. It had taken Chin Yeo to help him adjust and learn to survive the changes and learn his animal. All this retrospection needed to stop. His gut tightened. If he didn't find a damn distraction, the creatures would give him no rest. He wasn't ready to face her, not yet, he wasn't sure he had the strength. That fear had kept him alone all this time. He'd used it to protect his heart from the truth. The truth his dragons accepted and he fought, layering it with guilt and need, while chaos tore into his mind.

Silent, he paced the floor, letting the fire die down. The chill of the night crept into the cabin. As with every time this fight surfaced, he lost. There was no winner, because he didn't have an opponent. Regina was never there and the words he put in her mouth changed with every imagined dialogue.

He wasn't a talker, he needed action. He needed her touch, because late at night, like this night, he was so damned alone. Wounded, compromised and in the darkness, he admitted that much. Even if it didn't change his mind about heading west. He stopped at the door, looking over his shoulder at the laptop. This was a new fight though, and he'd need a tight wrap to get in and get out with his heart and soul intact.

He was not the same man who'd held her while she slept, shared his history with her, ate popcorn and watched movies with her cuddled next to him in the short time they'd been together. He was a creature of legend and nightmare, a man hardened by life and experience. She was a beauty to his beast and he determined to leave her free of his complications.

The thought didn't sit well with his wilder side. The dragons fought his reasoning, divided his rationale. He would release them and let them tire. The arguing would cease and he would sleep. There was no one solution to this fight, he'd come to that conclusion long ago.

He slipped out of his clothes and put the laptop to sleep. He was out the door in the darkness, another shadow in the shifting mists that give the Great Smoky Mountains their name. With a great cry, he shifted forms and leaped away from the gravity of the earth. His wings brushed the treetops, pulling him higher, reaching clear air. His mind tangled in memories, wondering how she made it, shuddered at the horror of roasting alive. Her tears falling hot on his skin, the fear that had consumed her, her grief at his death, all gut-punched him. He roared into the night, his own emotions too big to hold inside anymore.

Once the dam broke and everything rushed free, there was no barrier to protect him. His heart wrenched in his chest, causing very real pain as it struggled to absorb the regret. His feelings for Regina, feelings he'd shut off, shut down, locked away, swirled through him like poison, curdling his blood. His soul shriveled. He needed her, loved her and he'd deserted her when she needed his support most.

When his wings were too tired to stroke, he returned to his cabin. Coming down hard, he changed forms in flight. His body crashed into the clearing, knocking the breath out of him. The speed sent him tumbling across the open area, ass-over-head. He settled into the damp grass when the momentum exhausted itself, his heart thudding against his ribs, the double tattoo slowing to settle down. His breathing followed, while his mind heard the soft voice of Chin Yeo. The fire of his arousal banked and settled deep within him. If he couldn't have her, the one, his mate, he wanted nothing to do with his traitorous body. He shivered in the dew, body heat leaching out of his human skin.

Mitch rose to his hands, then to his feet. He stumbled with exhaustion. The cabin waited for him, its door open, as he'd left it in his mad scramble to use the adrenalin in his system. He staggered into the room and locked the door behind him. Making it up to the loft took the last of his strength, and for once he fell asleep without the insane urge for sex wracking his body. She followed him into deep slumber, a haunting question keeping him from restful sleep.

What if she didn't want him back in her life, could he walk away?

Three days later, Mitch used a cloth to work the rifle pieces on his kitchen table. The smell of gun oil filled his sinuses. It drowned the memory of another scent, almost. The door had opened and he recalled every nuance of her. She accompanied his every waking moment, but worse were the nights when she took over his mind. There was no sleep. When his body shut down, forcing the issue, there was only Regina.

He resolutely, without wasted emotion, boxed that memory and locked it behind a big armored door again. He'd performed the mental exercise so often it was unconscious, knowing it would not stay there. He knew it wouldn't hold. It hadn't for the lifetime since the email, the new mission specifications. He'd tried to rebottle the genie that was Regina. Nothing so far had worked. She hovered in his mind, a shade he couldn't banish. He had to settle for ignoring it. That wasn't working so well, either.

He stroked the black barrel, making sure every millimeter gleamed with oil, protected, ready for use, dependable. That mindless task he focused on so tightly he pushed all thoughts from his head of the one body that fit his, as precisely as the barrel of this gun fit the stock.

His biceps flexed as he stroked the blued length of steel. The finer muscles in his hands and wrists twitched with minimal movements as he reassembled the rifle. As muscle memory took over, his mind shut down. He could still assemble the rifle blindfolded without a hitch. He glanced at the laptop on the floor between his feet. Each member of his team eventually logged on, acknowledging his summons.

Jacob "Jake" Tobias was always first. He monitored the website for the team, kept this address encrypted. Mitch did not understand too much about it, he did not need to. He had Jake. Over six feet tall and slender, Jake carried his two hundred thirty-odd pounds all over. He spent his down time at the gym, in between fencing and martial arts. Mitch would have thought the loss of one eye would handicap Jake. One side of his mouth lifted, caught in the same scar, but it was not a smile. Jake kept on ticking.

"Boss man, this ain't nothing. I have patches for every occasion." He'd pointed at the side of his face. A bold scar slashed from his brow to the corner of his mouth. "This is a real pirate look. The chicks love it."

A soft tone let him know that Trevor joined them. He glanced out the window. Trevor must have been out biking or at the range. He wanted to be as good as the arrow-shooting elf in a series of movies. Trevor Kinkaid never went anywhere without a bow and whatever missile he needed to be deadly. His skills with a good old-fashioned knife were nothing to snort over, but he loved those bows of his.

A little guy, only five and a half feet tall, he dressed out at about one hundred fifty pounds. Scary fast, he looked like the kind of kid you paid to mow the lawn. A little geeky and shy, he used that as a lure for his particular type of woman, the ones who wanted to teach and train him. At thirty-six, he should be tired of that game. Evidently, it never got old.

Mitch sighed. He was tired tonight, weighed down with responsibility, heart sore, soul deep aching. Two more team members made it about the same time, Cox and Dughan.

Manuela "Manny" Cox loved detonations. He wondered what she was doing today. Manny probably spent her day mixing her own cocktails, testing them in her lab. Her ass length hair, braided to keep out it of her eyes, always came loose as she worked. Her five foot seven inch frame, too short to be model tall was still model formed. Slight, only a hundred and twenty pounds or so, her physique strengthened by free weights and, speed training with sparring partners, kept her body hard. She adopted the newest martial arts discipline, which used one's own animal instincts and adrenalin to make one unpredictable and deadly.

Mitch mused about that for an instant. She chose to be what he once loathed in himself.

Dughan. Hell if Mitch knew what to classify him. Well, to be fair, he did know what kind of witchcraft he practiced. A natural born witch from a long line of witches, he played with the elements. He manipulated the forces of the earth. It was the other talents Dughan had that defied any easy classification. His psi scores were so far off the charts the doctors could not read them. In practical review very little escaped him. What he didn't see, he sensed. Mitch shook his head. Dughan was their "pretty boy".

He'd modeled through college, where he attended medical school. The experience of being ogled as so much flesh without human recognition caused him to make himself literally invisible. Dughan did not believe he was there, so he was not. A good skill to have, but one often presenting a challenge in operations.

Benjamin Dughan stood six foot four and was a buff and deeply cut two hundred thirty-five pounds of man. Useful, irreplaceable, funny as hell, team medic, he was a reject of the foster care system.

The last piece snapped into place on the rifle. Mitch loaded each bullet. He checked each shell, gently rolling it into the clip. He locked the clip, chambered a round, set the safety. He stood to settle the weapon into its foam cradle. Securing the case, he wiped his hands on a dry rag on the table in front of him.

Another stray thought passed through his mind, wishing he were as together as the precision instrument of death he tucked away. The thought then raced away. He was every bit an instrument of destruction, probably the finest the military ever made. Leading these task force operations was where he was the best at what he did. It was in the day-to-day living that his flaws showed.

Chapter 17

He did not have time for this. Mitch shook his head, freeing his thoughts of the maudlin introspection, and picked up the laptop. That had happened too often while he awaited notice of action. Sighing, he clipped the all-seeing eye to the lip of his computer. Everyone else was settling down online, looking at split screen feeds of each other. He lifted his finger to key the command to link them, but he paused. He studied his team once more.

Jake sipped one of his endless energy drinks since he'd been online most of the day. When Jake joined the 'net he rarely backed out until one of his preset timers kicked him off.

Surrounded by graphite rods, apothecary jars of various things, probably all of them natural poisons used on the tips of his hand-balanced missiles, Trevor worked as he waited for the briefing. An air filter rested under his chin. The rubber straps cut into the side of his face. The adhesive used in the production of his arrows was strong enough to warrant the extra precautions. It must be raining in his area of the South to keep him inside.

Cox, her hair wispy around her head, eyes locked on her screen, studied a formula only she could see. Her high cheekbones wore smut from repeated swipes of her sooty hands. She was still busy, hating the interruption, waiting for his arrival.

He moved to Dughan, last team member to join both the team and the conference. He suppressed a start to find Ben's gaze locked on his through the terminal. His eyes accessing, his features even, his mood curious, Ben seemed to aim his dark gray gaze to probe through to Mitch.

Mitch hit connect to put him online. He tested his mental shields, there were no leaks, so Ben was trying to feel him out, not actually get inside the chaos that existed between his ears. *Time to focus, to get back on track.*

"Evening, everyone." His voice sounded rough and rusty. He ignored it. It would moderate with time and use. He would never again speak with the tones of a couple of years ago, since the damage of breathing fire on his vocal cords was irreversible. "New mission." Everyone watched him with varying degrees of enthusiasm.

"We have an incident to police in our own backyard. So far it hasn't leaked to the press or the international community. We want to keep it that way." He glanced around his screen.

"As you can see, dossiers are loading to your computers as we speak. Look them over. I want everyone to operations base by oh-nine-hundred tomorrow. Save your questions and make your arrangements. We will leave immediately after mission briefing." He watched every acknowledgment. As he reached to disconnect the conference, storm gray eyes made him pause. Ben's voice rang in his head, a warning or a curse, he did not know. Two words delivered with the echo of his fear and anticipation.

"She's there."

Mitch disconnected his link, blacking out his computer with a hand that shook. How had Dughan penetrated his shields? No matter how strong Ben happened to be, Mitch knew his shields to be stronger. How did Dughan know of her?

He watched the tremors in his hands, blending breathing with control until those telltale signs disappeared. He deepened his breathing and relaxed further, moving out of his chair and over to the clear space in the official dining room. Lack of furniture created his exercise floor.

Mitch removed his boots, setting them side by worn side away from the center. He unbuttoned and unzipped the BDUs wrapped around his hips, the rustle as they gathered around his ankles loud. His shirt peeled off his body to join the pile.

Nude, unencumbered, he moved into the blind time between day and night, his shadows a fluid silhouette. The repetition of steps old as time brought some of the physical chaos under his control. The tremors eased and then disappeared. His heart settled the restless rush in his chest. His movements smooth, gliding, kissed by starlight, amounted to controlled violence, bringing him peace.

As Mitch wove the intricate steps his breathing slowed more, the riot of his heartbeat forced to follow until the noise in his head became words. He worked his body in complete silence. Not a footfall whispered on the bare floor. Sweat rolled down his straining body, simply silent runnels of exertion. He worked until the moon cleared the trees in the backyard, limning his body with her silver touch.

He blinked in surprise at the light shining on him. When he finally relaxed the hold on his mind and body a glance at the clock on the wall showed him three hours were gone. He came to a stop, his muscles trembling with fatigue, his mind numb. He grabbed his clothes and boots, used his t-shirt as a towel to mop his face, and headed upstairs to the bedroom.

A shower soothed his body. He refused to wake his mind beyond lather, rinse and repeat. Stumbling to the bedroom, he fell into bed. His body worn out and his mind blocked, he slept.

The ranch in the desert looked no different from the way it had a lifetime ago, the first time he'd seen it. The very sight of it so close sent his heart into overdrive and woke the Drakken to pace under his skin. His team joined him at the door, ready to move in. He was thankful the base's security was so lax, or the invaders too busy to see them. The lack of a moon tonight aided them in their approach. Tricked out in the latest stealth gear and everyone with their favorite goodies at hand, they swept into the building.

Mitch searched the house, finding not one thing out of place, except no one was home. The kitchen was dark as the rest of the house, no mouthwatering smell of bread baking greeted him this time. The basement CCTV room was recording the desert and the house, including the elevator down and the landing at the top of the facility *Below*. Jacob reviewed the digital records, trying to find how big a force they would face.

Mitch waited patiently to see what they were up against before they loaded onto that elevator to hell. His team waited silently, focused on Jake and any info he could get them.

"We have four raiders, automatics, bandoliers with flash-bang. Two unknown men, can you ID?" He directed this to Mitch. Having lived down here, Mitch was the go-to for this directive more than anyone else. Mitch leaned into the screens.

"No, not our personnel, looks like scientists or doctors, no uniforms. Persons of interest, print us hardcopies to study." Mitch searched the screens himself, looking for a glimpse of her. The labs were empty, the morgue showed six bodies thrown in haphazardly, looked like some of the invading forces got what they deserved.

He wondered what happened to the last team, the six men still standing when the lights went on.

"Jake, see if the lower levels six and seven are active. That was the last training field. If we have any luck at all, those will be in our control and all we have to do is make it down there." He watched as Jake pulled those levels up and then checked archived hours in fast forward.

The grind of the printer stopped and Mitch handed the pics over to the rest of the team. "Subdue and capture, folks," he told them, his gaze intently roaming the screens.

"Here you go," Jake told Mitch. Together they watched the infiltration. It was easy for the invaders once they had the house. Using the elevator and stopping at each level, they cleared them out. It appeared they locked the lift until they secured that level. Lower, the incumbent soldiers kept the four-man force very busy, busy enough for them to have called in reinforcements.

They watched another team of six enter the ranch and descend. Joining the living three invaders, they wasted no time securing the remaining floors. Then they reached the fifth level where the incumbent forces were hell bent on defense.

Unfortunately, the upper floors were civilian and included the operational functions of the base. Once the third and fourth levels were breached, the onsite employees were herded like cattle to the lower floor. Using the civilians against the bivouacked troops, they gained the upper hand, decimating the guard forces.

Down one floor to the living quarters, they strode the corridors, rousting the technicians and doctors out of their rooms and into the halls. There the civilians milled around, waiting for decisions. The workers were released to return to their apartments, labs and above with an escort.

His mind worked on different levels. The situation wasn't right. If they released techs and civilians to higher levels, how did they know the base personnel wouldn't run? That meant they'd somehow locked down the base so there was no escape. They were watching the ranch for any breach.

"We're under surveillance. Jake, make sure you sweep this area, they know the civilians haven't escaped."

"So they're watching the house for any movement." Jake bent under the array and Mitch heard a zipper. He straightened with a small device in his hand, passing it to Ben.

"Know how to work this?" At Ben's nod he turned back to the array, typing quickly into the mainframe. A screen began to scroll gibberish to Mitch and he moved away. Crossing his arms over his chest, he watched Ben scan the room and then move into the hallway with Trevor following him.

His body needed air. His lungs expanded, drawing in a slow breath. He wasn't aware he'd stopped breathing when fear shut down his body as he searched for her.

There was no sign of Regina or the other team on any of the screens. He stopped the feelings of loss trying to crowd into his mind. His stomach returned to normal, hard won discipline coming to his rescue. Lower the scans went as Jake investigated every level.

Finally getting to the floor with the training center, Mitch moved back to Jake's side. The team he worked with, the last six men, were still there. They had to be. There was a complete scene of butchery at the elevator door on level seven.

Mitch and Jake watched the military attack as soon as the door opened, somehow separating the civilian fodder from the militaristic invaders. With a few weapons, but mostly hand to hand, they pulled the attack force from the elevator before the doors closed and tore them apart.

A flash bang went off, blinding the camera for a brief time. When the smoke cleared, no one was moving except for the defending team. Then into the frame she appeared. Slipping into triage mode, she checked for any signs of life, moving quickly from one body to another. Shaking her head, she looked over the team. One wounded she motioned to a door down the hall.

She looked around her at the mess, gathered the uninjured and put them to work cleaning. They followed her directions. No one hesitated. Not one spoke out against her. The civilians, shoved back into the elevator when the welcoming party started, returned to the upper levels. All were happy to go.

The rest of the men with Regina made short work of cleaning up the area. Each one made his way into the gym, where an office turned surgery gleamed under bright lights. He watched in fast forward as she patched and sewed, smiling and coaxing the men down from their aggressiveness.

It had been a remarkable sight. Even in normal mode the attack had taken no time, the incredible reflexes of his last team propelled them double time. The invaders hadn't stood a chance against them. They worked together, a single unit of death.

The raiders regrouped on the upper level, showing Mitch and his team their total number at nine. This would have been at midnight, the night before this night.

"I wonder if they've lost any more," Jake mused into the silence.

"Let's figure not." Mitch straightened, eyeing his team.

"We found several stick ups." Trevor dumped the small cameras onto the table in front of Jake. He picked up one and turned it over in his hand, studying it. Mitch waited.

"They're cheap and throwaway."

"Do they work?" Mitch picked up one.

"They warned that we were here and how many we are. I can't see where there is any communications added to them." He looked at Ben. "Did you find any mics?"

"Nothing to listen." Ben shook his head.

"Then they know we're here and we're coming, but they don't know the plan." Everyone looked at Mitch. He tossed the camera to the table with a sigh.

"There is a way down into this facility through the air ducts. It ain't pretty or easy. The end of the line is in the morgue." He looked around with a mean curve to his lips. "Anybody have an issue?"

"Aw, Mitch, do I hafta go?" Jake whined behind the console.

"You sound like a spoiled five year old, get your ass out of that chair. It's time to get dirty," Trevor scolded. His face reflected his anticipation of action and he rubbed his hands together, excitement in every movement.

"I hate dirty," Manny Cox told them deadpan, picking imaginary dirt from her nail.

It had the desired effect when everyone laughed. Already Manny's hair was floating loose of the braid, her face was smudged from collecting dust and sweating on their way in.

Ben threw an arm around her. "That's our diva, never a hair out of place."

"I think she looks like Pigpen, you know, on that cartoon? He carried a blanket? Dust flew around him?" Every question rose higher in tone as Trevor took his shot at her.

Manny cut her gaze to the one who could have been her twin.

"Payback will be hell, that's a promise." She dropped her

backpack to rearrange the load, not wanting to carry too much heavy duty. They were below ground and she did not want to collapse the mine-like tunnels.

The rest of them discarded anything they could do without and readied themselves to crawl down the access route. Joking all done, for now, they found a locker hidden in the kitchen and stored the extras there. No one was likely to check cabinets. They could grab their stuff quickly on the way out.

Mitch had promised them it was not easy. Even with advanced knowledge of the way in it was messy. More than one of his team was bleeding when they finally dropped into the morgue. Regrouping, they headed out of the morgue and down the corridors.

Mitch presumed the biggest part of the raiding force would be in the labs, trying to decipher the work of Gardner and Laurel. If he could free the six men from the gym levels his force would more than double.

"They may be in the conference room." They had not passed anyone friend or foe in the corridor.

"If there is any information left there, collect it. We may need all the clues we can gather to fix this travesty." Mitch warned them of the possible reception before he opened the door. He moved them to either side of the wall, keeping them out of the line of fire. He took a position in the center doorway.

Chapter 18

The door opened, bringing him face to face with two of his original team. He waited, not moving, for them to recognize him. He had changed in the time away.

"Commander, is that you? Why are you here? What brought you back?" One of the men stepped to him cautiously, his steps freezing when he glimpsed others flanking his former commander.

"We've been sent to get you out." Mitch stepped into the doorway, blocking both teams from attack. "How long have they been down here? What has happened since they invaded? How much do you all know about them?" He fired off the questions, battling a sudden rise of guilt. Many of the answers he already knew. Like the man in front of him, he knew it was almost impossible to repair shattered trust.

"We don't know how long they were down here, searching level by level. They are some off- shoot extremist faction of the religious community in control of one of their holy lands. We don't understand much of what they say. They have made one try down this far, we held them off." He paused to clear his throad, falling into classical defrief to catch his superior officer up to speed.

"Doc Reggie came down with us when you died." The man finished his report on a purely personal note. There was a break in his voice, echoes of hell roughing the tone.

"Well, we thought you died. When we came back out the lights were still bright. You and the others were gone. Everything was cleaned up nice and pretty.

"Dr Regina moved in with us, keeping us under observation, using the lights for seconds at a time, helping us—" He finally saw a body move in the hallway. The soldier, his name Moody according to the name on his uniform, jumped back into a fighting stance.

"Who you got with you, Commander?" He eyed the hallway behind Mitch. There was a pause while the two defenders looked around at the team now standing behind Commander Bolton.

133

"Moody, meet your rescue." Mitch stepped aside, allowing one at a time to step from the wall and stand in the corridor. "This is Jake, Trevor, the biggest of them is Ben, then our never delicate diva, Manny Cox."

"Nice to meet you." Moody watched them file into the hallway. He stared at them, all arranged in the corridor. "Come on in, might as well take a seat." He stepped back, allowing them past, then he leaned into the hallway.

"Commander, you didn't use the elevator?" he asked, eyes still roaming the assembled team.

"No. They have it locked on one of the upper levels."

"Good. That way we have warning they're headed down here." Moody motioned to the elevator. "How did you make it down?"

Mitch stepped in, allowing Moody to close the door behind him. For better or worse, they were *Below*. All he had to do now was figure a way to get them all together, the good guys and the bad guys and the guys who were barely either.

"We came through the air system." He looked around the room, now too small for the people grouped inside.

"Moody, is there a place we can meet and set up a roster and plan of action?" Mitch remembered only the office and the observation level. He knew this double level also held a kitchen, coolers, quarters, a full morgue and the gym.

"Of course, Commander, if you'll follow me we can go to the dining room. It should work fine." Moody turned and led them down the corridor. One by one Mitch's team fell in behind the soldier, matching steps, keeping silent. When they arrived at the dining room Mitch found it to be larger than he remembered. It would comfortably sit fifty to seventy-five people. Already there at a table, three of the other soldiers were laughing. When they saw Mitch they jumped to attention. He remembered to tell them at ease.

"Let me explain some things. Is this everyone?" Moody, Adams, Williams, and Conway watched the others settle at another table. Moody nodded.

"Everyone who is mobile." Moody looked at his table. "We almost lost Carlisle, and Hanover will be back on his feet later."

"Good to see you guys are still alive." Mitch told them sincerely, shaking hands and accepting hugs from the mixed bag of military. Their probable elimination had haunted him. They nodded, silent acknowledgement of what their future could have held.

"I'm not military any more. However, I am in charge of getting you free and safe from the invaders upstairs. I do not know the status of this lab or the contents therein. I do not know what orders have come down for you from Washington." Mitch settled at the head of the table. What came next was going to be the most difficult. And the explanation needed to be heard. He felt he owed it to the remaining team members.

"I escaped the horror the day of our birth. I made it through the desert, met up with some mercenaries, made my way with them until I was rescued by our forces overseas and shipped back as MIA. No one at any time referred to my time here or what transpired before I escaped.

"Some of you may have discovered some different traits due to your exposure to certain lighting and the serum. I completely understand. If by some miracle you escaped these traits and keep with the Jekyll and Hyde affect that is cool, too." He turned to Moody.

"Moody, you were telling me that Doc Reggie was helping you all adjust and control the beast inside, am I right?" Moody glanced at the others gathered, the new force and his teammates. They looked back at him, some clueless and others sharing the months of fear and adjustment. Moody nodded.

"Is there anything else she could be working on that might help? Specifically, has she found another serum or vaccine to stop this process?"

Moody shook his head.

Adams spoke. "Commander, it is irreversible. I've heard Doc Reggie say that a lot. We have it and we are going to have to live with it. If we don't get too tense, we don't experience so much of it, you know?" He glanced at the others in the room. He was not the only one hiding the true horror behind vague phrases. Mitch was not sure he wanted his new team to know the full story, either.

"Got it, so other than light, are there any other triggers?"

"Anger, frustration, hunger, real hunger not the growling belly hungry, extremes in emotions will trigger us," Williams told Mitch as he stood to get more coffee. "You would think the amount of caffeine we consume would do it, but that seems to be as safe as always."

Mitch smiled. He'd discovered that himself. The military machine ran on caffeine. You could take yourself out of the military life, but it was hard as hell to take the caffeine need out of you.

"How about the head?"

Williams turned, his eyes searching Adams then moving to Mitch. Conway joined the conversation.

"The head is still strong," he affirmed. Conway was a marine, if Mitch remembered. The mix of services was less obvious *Below,* because each had worn the same BDUs. Only a small badge denoted the official branch of service, and it was optional. Most of the men *Below* had stopped wearing it after a week or so of their arrivals, becoming a true team in the project.

Conway's eyes held the shadows created when he blew the lizard man apart in self-defense. His mental defense kicked in without forethought. He answered the unasked question in Mitch's gaze. "Those are integrated, last resort measures. Doc Reggie has been with us twenty-four/seven since that day. We discovered a few things since then."

Mitch wanted to see Dr. Regina Gardner, in a bad way. He wanted to know if she was holding up, since the last picture he had of her was grainy and distressing. Yet his job was to purge the lab, and his mind hadn't reconciled the monster with the creation.

"Mitch, we have a window, man. I don't know what the double language you guys are using means, but we need to hustle and cap this place before they decide to strike us down and turn this into one big glass tube," Trevor spoke up.

"I'm not forgetting that, Trevor." Mitch thought for a moment. "Adams, correct me if I'm wrong, but isn't there a communications array down here?"

"Yes, sir, at the other end of the corridor. We use it to communicate with the upper levels. Since the day you di–left us, this has been home. When we need things we send for them and the elevator brings them down." Adams nodded his head in the general direction.

"Jake, see what you can find out. Block all out going signals. You know the drill. I want radio silence to be our message to our *ears.* Then let's see if we can find our quarry, one by one." Mitch turned to Manny.

"Cox, got any petite surprises in your bag of tricks? Something small enough to clean out the freight box, but leave the elevator functional?" He watched her review her mental list.

"I think I have one or two that would work, Boss. If not, it should be easy to cobble something up with my supplies." She smiled, bearing white teeth, in a grin that wasn't pleasant.

"Trevor, think you could find a place to hide in the freight box, maybe stash a few trigger toys, in case?" Mitch played to the strengths of each of them. Putting them to work would ease the growing nerves, set them up for eventual success, and get them away from any slip in information he wanted to keep private.

"Oh yeah, Boss. Let me at it." Trevor shot to his feet. "Come on, Pigpen. Let's go check out the elevator." He looked at Manny, who was not smiling now.

"So help me." She stood slowly as she looked at the rest of her teammates. "If that asinine name sticks to me, you will all pay." Manny Cox was serious. If they did not want exploding toothbrushes or itching powder in toilet paper the name would disappear. Those were merely a few of the scars Manny's promises had left on their psyches.

Each of them nodded solemnly, even Mitch. When she turned to face Trevor, he smiled and pulled her out of the room, busy talking a mile a minute about things that go boom. He was never affected by her threats, even as he bore the brunt of the outcome. His nature kept the unafraid smile on his lips. Mitch didn't know if he was lacking in self preservation instincts or if he put up with Cox because there was a deeper affection.

Mitch shook his head at their antics. Jake left with Adams, heading for communications. Ben moved with his coffee to the table with Conway, Williams and Moody. Mitch joined them. Moody shifted seats away from Williams, and with a slight hesitation, Ben took the seat. Williams nodded at Ben, recognition flaring in his gaze before a smile swept his lips upward.

"In case you missed it, we have an eight hour window to find and secure the raiders. If we don't make it, this facility will be put on full security override and then bombed with bunker busters until the sand turns to glass, trapping everyone down here until death us do part," Mitch finished, taking the last dregs of cool coffee.

"That's laying it all on the table." Moody shook his head.

"I was afraid that had already happened here. When everything went to hell that day, the military was well within the rights to stop the contagion." Mitch took Ben's coffee and sipped the cooling brew.

"Shit, they ran like little kids when the bogey man showed up." Moody growled in a low tone. "So much for their support during the trials." He sat back and crossed his arms. "They left us alone. There was so much—"

"I remember. I was catatonic, in a way. My mind was working but I couldn't move, couldn't talk, couldn't fight." Mitch admitted. Into the grim silence Conway cleared his throat, ending that conversation.

"How can we help?" Conway asked. "I remember looking at schematics for these levels on the computer station in my quarters. Assuming the units all work off a master/slave set up, we should be able to access them and find a way out of here without using the elevator."

"Or the air ducts." Ben refilled the cups, rubbing his hip where he'd sustained a nasty welt on the way down.

"Right, the civilians wouldn't be effective going up the levels that way. It would take days."

"The office on the observation deck should be able to access them," Moody offered. "It depends on the biohazard defenses down here. Remember, this was set up for things like anthrax and other airborne infections. If it gets triggered while we are climbing through a vent or access tunnel, the defenses may wipe us out before the enemy does."

"I had forgotten that," Mitch mused, nodding. He'd made it through the air ducts easily. Now he wondered if those defenses were actually live. Coming down the ducts with his team hadn't triggered anything, but he hadn't expected it to. The defenses were set to kill any escape of contagions, not watching for invasions.

"Maybe I can help." Ben joined the discussion. "If I can find the labs on this level I may be able to access security parameters and disable those I can get to."

"Moody, Ben. Ben, Moody. Let's get started." Mitch looked at Conway and Williams.

"I don't know what we can do to help. I certainly don't want to send you up without defenses. Let's find those schematics. Maybe we can get to their scientists and capture them without any fuss and then get everyone the hell out of here." He motioned for Moody to lead the way out. The teams split in the hall.

Chapter 19

Regina sewed up Hanover, checked on Carlisle and retreated to her quarters. Standing in front of the fan, she undressed to the skin. It was always too hot for her now. The cooling unit in her rooms was down as far as it could go. Luckily, the thermostat went down to forty degrees. She was more comfortable in the refrigeration temperatures. Something happened to her with the serum and she had yet to discover the key to correcting her body's symptoms.

Cold equaled rest. Her body overheated too easily since the serum integrated with the adjustments caused by Dr. Laurel's final injections. Wishing she had the strength to send him to hell, she stretched out on her bed with another box fan pushing the cold air against her. She gave up on tears a long time ago, resigning herself to living down here. When Dr. Laurel found out about the changes in her biology, he laughed and wished her luck.

Regina had begun showing symptoms within two hours of the disaster in the gym. Laurel had checked her out.

"It appears to me the serum is changing your biochemistry. It is responding differently from the way it does males." He tipped her head back, shining a light into her eyes, searching. "How do you feel?" Stepping back, he crossed his arms over his chest.

"Nauseous and gagging on the taste of betrayal." She grasped the edges of the exam bed, keeping her claws from his face, her hands from gripping his neck. "I'm feverish, temperature climbing."

"Yet your white cells are not responding as if to an infection." He'd insisted on taking blood, and now was she sorry she'd allowed him to have it. Who knew what he would use it for in the future? She'd been so worried with her responses to the light and about the men she'd agreed to any test he suggested.

"I really thought it would make you a new woman." Shaking his head, he pulled the stethoscope from his neck, looping the tube around his hand. "I really like you, Regina. It saddens me that you took up with the military against me. He had no right to you."

"You are mental." She hadn't known his feelings for her. Not that she'd have returned them. Her heart skipped a beat, refusing to continue without Mitch. He'd died and she had learned before this examination that his body was in the crematory oven, baking to ash and bones.

"You were perfect, the perfect subject. You were an angel waiting for discovery, for a new birth with the serum. You would have been a modern Valkyrie, an Amazon." He stepped close to her. "I would have made you a queen in my kingdom." He whispered, one hand incautiously drifting over her breast.

Regina slapped his hand. Her other hand punched him hard enough to send him staggering back.

"You sick son of a bitch. I would never go with you. Touch me again and I'll kill you." She moved off the table and to the door, staggering weakly. "I know you have plans to leave. I'd get going. The men aren't going to be as forgiving as I am." There was no absolution in her voice.

Arrogant, he rubbed his crotch, drawing her attention to his erect cock. Her stomach roiled. She wasn't strong enough mentally or physically to deal with this, not so soon after the consecutive shocks of the day. She bolted from the room, leaving behind his taunting laughter.

Then he'd left the labs, the chaos and death after he'd cleansed the area and packed his findings. It hadn't taken him long.

All the months later Regina never gave up. In her lab she worked tirelessly on viral carriers to correct the effects. When she believed they had it isolated and deliverable, the carrier broke down, or the body attacked the virus before it could infect and start the repair process.

Tracy and Mike worked with her, only they had stayed after the last trial was complete. Tracy because of Adams, the soldier she'd given her heart to. He'd survived and they spent every minute together after the close call.

Mike followed her example, bonding and then moving in with Gareth Hanover, a sailor who'd been proud to be picked for the mission. From a medical background, he'd studied beside Mike since the bloody day, using his knowledge to suggest other avenues to correct what happened. A man in love, Mike couldn't work hard enough. Gareth sometimes physically pulled him from the lab and took him home to food and rest.

Regina rolled to her back, finding another cooler spot to stretch, wishing her mind would shut down and let her rest. She'd relived those moments so often the memories tore at her until she wanted to scream. Inside her something twisted, fighting for freedom, the strength of it frightening. She feared this part of her, fearsome and primal inside from her infection.

Regina would never forget that day, the day Mitch didn't make it through. Seeing his body strapped to a stretcher heading for the morgue had made her want to die with him. Less than an hour later the site went into lockdown. Dr. Laurel and all the research they developed together was packed in boxes, downloaded to disks, and sent topside.

Many of the support personnel added to take care of the increased population evacuated. The base went into sleeper mode and few people remained here. Yet those still living at the time remained incarcerated below, held back from escape by men with loaded weapons and cold eyes. Excellent examples of "friendly fire".

It was too late to send out her information, and without Mitch, she simply didn't know who would want it. She packed all of it into a secure place and tried to take care of her grief. There were times she knew Mitch hadn't died, that somehow he'd survived and would be back to get her. Then she remembered his eyes looking up at her from his dead face. They'd been different, the pupil elongated. He'd not had a heartbeat, not a breath lifted his chest where she most wanted to throw herself.

She wished she had allowed herself to say good-bye, allowed the closure that she needed for sanity. But she'd held back, thinking he was invincible and somehow he'd figure a way back to her, for her. The changes in his DNA became obvious as he'd been changing when he'd died. Attendants had stood beside his body, eager to take him to the morgue.

She could still hear the horrible words of the mad scientist. "This has been a wonderful trial. A final success."

"How can you say that?"

The memory of Laurel grasping her arm, likely the only reason she didn't throw herself onto Mitch's corpse. She flung her arm away at the memory. Anger surged through her, twining with the grief overwhelming her. Tears choked her, tears she couldn't shed. She'd be twice damned before she'd show a weakness to this bastard.

"The adjustment I made to the serum was successful. It will be a very marketable product. I expect the efficiency to carry over for some time, if not permanently."

"All you cared about was the money?" She'd known it, and yet still hadn't wanted to admit it. Something moved under her skin, slinking toward the surface, anger in every sinuous movement. She battled it back, finding again her trust broken and her rosy view of the world very dark and bleak.

"I worked damn hard for every nuance of the formula, put my team through hell and back, and all you were thinking was about the payday?" She jerked from his hold, pacing the floor beside the gurney holding her lost heart. "What about the men you murdered, the ones left here?"

"They were very helpful. As were you and your endeavors. My dear, this was always about the bottom line." He stopped her pacing and waving the gurney forward, he pulled her close. "All except you. How do you feel?"

Her skin crawled. "How am I supposed to feel?" It was everything Mitch told her, coming at her like a runaway freight train heading for a wall.

"My dear, you've been a participant. I need to check you over. You don't seem to have the aggression levels of the males." It was how she'd found herself in his exam room, listening to him brag and catalogue her health as part of the program.

"The first two teams showed signs of deterioration. Their genetics fought with their sanity. In actual testing, they became animalistic killing machines. After turning on each other, we realized they needed a leader. Unfortunately, Mitch Bolton was the last trial team, so he wasn't present to pull them back to a functioning unit." His voice was oily, sticking to her as he calmly recited the information she and Mitch seen but hadn't breathed to another soul. He knew everything about the killing.

"It was the single worse military tragedy in history. On a routine training mission, the lights went out and the troops training got confused and lost their way. One wrong move and they opened fire. All twenty men were killed in that deadly crossfire." Regina could accept his despair if he'd delivered the statements with any honesty. She shivered at his careless delivery of the news.

"You're a cold hearted bastard." Even as she said the words to Laurel, it wasn't strong enough to express what she felt for him. The aggression levels in her mind prepared her body for fight. She stood beside him, remembering her last view of Mitch as the stretcher team rolled Mitch down the hallway.

"And you, lovely one, are one of them now. I see you're repressing the instinct to attack. This should have been women only. The next set will be. The female of the species is stronger than the male."

"What happens next?"

"I would love to take you with me. I think that fire burning inside of you is incredibly arousing. But you would not follow my directions. I need to take this to the next step, find better vectors to carry it to mass numbers of people, soldiers, and hell, to entire villages.

"You would once have belonged to me, but the rumors of you and the Commander ruined that. Now, you're used goods, and even though you possess the strength to fight the killing rage, I will find another to prepare." He sneered down at her, distaste in his features. She was glad and horrified. She couldn't help Mitch, but she could help the others. If she could control the reactions, she would teach the team to control theirs.

Regina stayed or accepted banishment down here. She had some ideas. Something sent her to the gym where Mitch trained the teams. When she got there the six survivors of the team of ten were in shock. They showered, some of them until their bodies were water logged and scraped raw. She called Tracy for some tranquilizers, whatever they had in the veterinary closet. She made short work of dosing them and getting them to sleep. She monitored them, not willing to leave this last bunch of survivors alone.

As they woke she questioned them one by one. The story they told appalled her. It was beyond sane belief, but by then she was beginning to suffer the heat effects and could readily accept their stories. She asked if any of them were experiencing other symptoms of the change. No one spoke up, yet telling glances passed from man to man. If they were experiencing something profound, they would suffer it in silence. This was a tight team. They would keep this to their graves.

To help them she needed in, past the aggressive male soldier to the volunteers she'd treated for months, friends she'd made. Regina had her work cut out for her. She had to help them control the aggressive tendencies that emerged under the blood lights and not kill each other. It took minutes, then days and finally weeks passed under the blood lights, but the men all learned to control the aggression.

There were plenty of accidents along the way. Since she was closest to a medical doctor *Below* now staffed, the treatment fell to her. She learned more about the damage the human body could sustain than she'd ever wanted to know.

It took time for the walls to weaken and then fall. They gradually allowed her in and she pushed them to help her. While none of them changed form as they reported their teammate did, many of them experienced partial shifts.

Regina racked her memory, turning over rooms, trying to find every file Dr. Laurel left behind, in case there was a clue he overlooked, a hint of what direction she could go. It was a lucky break when Mike found the first of the information.

If ninety percent of the DNA chain comprised genetic material from all species, when Dr. Laurel chose starfish material for the regeneration factor, he actually activated reptilian aspects in the organ cell walls. Combined with the serum, it strengthened the incidence of body reformation, assisted by the higher than average psi abilities. While that explained the lizard man and some of the scaled, clawed appendages reported under duress by the men, it didn't go far with helping her find an antidote for them all.

By this time any prolonged exposure to the regular temperatures in the facility wore her out. She became dehydrated and finally succumbed. Waking once with her body packed in ice to bring down her fever, she had IVs attached to each arm and leg. That was the final straw. She renovated both her quarters and a singular workstation to help her continue to work in some comfort and safety.

She knew the staff and military worried about her. Looking at her as their only link to a cure or at least a remission, they were stymied by her new problems. While they were comfortable, she shivered. When they ate, she nibbled, her body fighting with her to accept the regular diet. Thank goodness their food supplies remained regular, their water and air supplied freely *Below* as though nothing had happened.

She modified her new quarters to provide her with a den, of sorts, where she could bring down her core temperature. She moved with the help of the men and settled close to them. A new team formed that include Regina as everyone involved realized the truth.

She'd walked into the cafeteria and found the rag tag team cooking for everyone now there were so few left.

Tracy stood in front of a table, holding court. "Doc Reggie is infected the same as all of you. She's suffering in a different way. Please take it easy on her. We're doing all we can to find a solution."

"What do you mean, she's infected?" Adams asked.

Regina held the door.

Tracy saw her but didn't give her away. "The mad scientist gave her the injections, telling her it was because we needed vitamin boosts for living out of the sunlight for so long."

"She believed him?"

"Remember, she's a linguist and research scientist. She knows and uses biology, but only to the extent that helps her with the study."

"Fuck."

Tracy nodded. There were other voices added to the harsh curse.

Before pandemonium broke out Regina made her presence known. "I'm okay." She worked quickly to assure the small gathering. "I don't have the sensitivity to the light and the aggression is manageable." More than one person stood to touch her, look closely at her, their wounds barely healed searching for hers.

"I swear I will do all I can to fix this mess, get us all back to whatever our normal will be."

Every day they woke up was a great day for the team. The protocol should be a full extermination. In the fine print of their contracts was the clause that covered the use of extreme prejudice should any or all of the laboratories fail. They waited daily for the end to find them, then the tension eased and they started to think they'd been abandoned, left to kill themselves into oblivion. A clean up team sent down to get rid of the remains and the base opened again for the next great project to receive funding never happened.

Regina made one last foray above level six on the day she moved her quarters and lab down two floors. Using the door code for Mitch's quarters, she slipped inside. For a long time she wandered around his space, touching the few things there that seemed personal. She checked his bedroom, as Spartan as his living spaces.

In the drawer of his nightstand, she found a ring box. Under the box was a receipt, dated the week before his cremation. Inside was a beautiful emerald ring her size. Maybe it was all supposition on her part, but she knew she loved him and believed he loved her. She took the pillows from his bed, carrying the faint scent of his cologne and the musky scent of his body, down to her rooms. When the door shut to her quarters, soft and final, she curled around his scent and cried herself to sleep. The ring box clutched to her breasts, she dreamed of all the good times between them.

She mourned him in the weeks that followed. Getting too little sleep and not enough food began to tell on her. Her lab assistants cajoled, offered and then forced her to eat. She worked like someone mad, and maybe she was a little crazed. Never in a million years would she have seen this turn of events, living underground like animals not allowed out of the burrow. Slowly her heart eased and the days were easier, the diverse personalities of her level mates lured her out of the shell of despair.

She'd been accepted by the brotherhood, a loose grouping of the survivors stretching to include Tracy and Mike.

The ring she wore on a chain around her neck. Like a promise of success, she kept Mitch close to her heart, vowing every night to find the answer to reverse the process. Every day she worked with the soldiers, helping direct the aggression. Making them stay under the filtered light longer and longer until they could handle themselves.

She remembered the cheering, the tears, when the lights came on and no one needed stitching up. They called for alcohol and cake and threw open the doors of the level for one hell of a party. Ignored by the higher levels, happy to be close family, they enjoyed the time free of interruption.

It was a normal day, normal for *Below* as they worked toward an answer to so many questions about their conditions. They'd been attacked out of the blue. Without any warning from above, the elevator opened. Instead of their requested supplies, behind a group of unexpected civilians, clearly hostages, men with guns jumped from the freight box and started firing into the waiting team. With a combined roar, the team surged forward, pushing and shoving the civilians out and down to the floor. They grabbed the weapons, tearing them from the invaders. As one they lined up, each taking a turn as they cleaned the box of attackers.

They left the bloody bodies where they lay, pushing the civilians back inside for the trip topside. A runner came for Regina, dragging her from another fruitless search for any answer. She noted the dead, fixed the minor wounds sustained in the defense and after a short surgery, allowed Carlisle to rest. His recovery should be complete in a day, a welcome side effect of the change in their DNA.

Regina rolled over and vowed to close her eyes for a minute. Exhaustion, like a shadow being attached to her body, took over and pulled her under. This new siege might be the beginning of the end, and if they couldn't find a way topside to escape, all of them would die here. Those dreams chased her through sleep.

Chapter 20

The five men entered the observation level. Mitch looked down at the scene of destruction belched from his memory. Revulsion still had the power to clog his throat, make his stomach clench. Williams laid a hand on his shoulder. Mitch blinked the memory away, seeing the pristine gym under the normal lighting.

"It's okay, man. We made it through all that. Doc Reggie helped us every day. Stitched us up when we got too rough, even held us when we cried. We can do it now. We can survive that light for a long time." He spoke so softly the others didn't hear.

Mitch nodded, his throat working as his Drakken roared for justice. He turned to the monitors, watching the schematics flash before him. Access tunnels would be the best choices. The halls were bigger circumferences, had easy floor-to-floor steps and ladders, so more people could move faster. It would still be cramped and uncomfortable.

"Mitch?"

He turned to see who called him as a short, plump bundle cannon-balled into him. Arms and legs wrapped around him, nearly taking him to the floor. He recognized her at the last second. She'd lost weight, but the exuberance and attitude were still there.

"Tracy, is that you?" He leaned away to see her smiling face.

"You bet! By damn, we thought you were dead. They took you to the morgue. What happened? Have you seen Regina? She's going to die!" Tracy spoke too fast for him to answer her questions.

"One at a time, Tracy." He chuckled as he eased her to the floor. "You look same as ever. I was not dead. I have not seen Regina." He relaxed enough for a real smile at her enthusiasm. Her excitement brushed away anguish returning *Below* brought up. She grinned at him, shaking her head in disbelief.

"Good to see you're still here. Which one of these soldiers is yours, anyway?" he asked her as they moved away from the computer station, lowering their voices. Tracy smiled and nodded her head toward Adams.

"They saved the best for last, but we nearly lost you all. Regina has been looking for a way to reverse this, but so far we can't seem to get it right." Tracy cast a worried glance at the men clustered around a monitor.

"We wait every day to be locked in and terminated. Sometimes the fear of it makes me sick." She shook herself as if shaking away the thoughts. Her smile broke free of the emotional tangle showing in her features. "Or maybe I'm pregnant." She leaned close and whispered. "But don't tell Jimmy, it's going to be a surprise." She paused for a breath, not long enough for him to congratulate her, them.

He thought about how he'd feel if Regina had his baby.

"Go see Regina," she urged him. "She's bunked down here with the rest of us, down that main corridor and off the left hallway. Her door is H15. You'll have to ring. We don't have key locks down here." Tracy watched him closely for a moment. She leaned close, lowering her voice, her gaze serious when it locked with his.

"Mitch, she grieved for you. For weeks she mourned." Tracy looked toward the men around the station behind him for a moment, then back to him. "She's got what they have, but different. She has to stay, well, refrigerated. We don't know what the serum and injections did to her female biology, but it wasn't a good thing."

She rose up to her tiptoes to reach his cheek almost ten inches above her. Smacking a quick kiss against his skin, she licked the desert and sweat off her lips with a grimace.

"Maybe you should stop by the showers first." Her eyes filled with shadows, the look far away from her smile. She turned and joined the crowd, asking if she could help. He watched Adams pull her to his side, tucking her close.

A quick trip to his old room and he knew that someone had taken Regina's ring. The emerald represented his promise to her, a promise of a future, and a successful end to the mess they were embroiled in. He wanted to tear up the joint.

A slow smile lifted the corners of his lips when he noticed his missing pillows. Regina would be the only one seeking comfort in his linens. His face tightened in pain and the loss she must have felt. He'd died twice, nothing could be harder than surviving that. His rebirth as a Drakken was nothing, he'd survived. This agonizing awakening of his heart he wasn't sure he'd live through.

He let the ties on his compartmentalized emotions loosen, slipping from the memories he'd tried to hold at bay. Want and need moved through him, waking the lightly sleeping Drakken. They strained close to the surface, excitement beginning to course through him, his heart beating faster. All this for a glimpse of her, the chance after all this time to speak with her, hold her. He turned his mind from that train of thought, unsure if he could restrain himself from taking their reunion to the fullness of their previous relationship.

The Drakken growled low, a muted noise in his head. They wanted to see their mate, touch her, and wake her. The animals had never seen her. He walked faster, unconsciously moving toward the end of yearning. He headed back down the access tunnel, avoiding cameras and listening close for footfalls. If he could get them all out that way...

But even if the lower level evacuated, the top levels would be a fight. They were going to have to clear them foot by foot. He didn't want to drag a bus load of civilians through a gun fight they were in no way prepared to participate in or survive. He reminded himself others were working on that solution, dropping it from his mind. He followed Tracy's directions to Regina's quarters.

Now he stood in front of the door, a web belt holding his pants up, thanks to the supplies no one had taken f from his quarters. The same quarters had also yielded BDUs, fresh as he could make them and inches too loose on his frame now. He lifted his hand to ring, hovering in midair. Hesitating, he rested his hand instead on the door itself. He wondered for a minute, as these doors were the same as military quarters if she would choose... Not a chance, he told himself.

With the same instinct that kept him alive, he keyed his old door code into her lock. The door whispered open. He walked into the room which felt to him like a deep freeze. The door closed behind him.

He didn't see her, but he spied a pile of her clothes jumbled on the floor. He walked down the short hall to the bedroom. On top of the covers, back turned to the door, Regina slept. His eyes followed every bone in her back, noting the lack of any extra weight on her body. The dimples at the base of her spine where her pert ass met her back were starvation hollows. Her hipbones showed white through her skin, which used to be a healthy cream and was now a sallow fish belly tone.

He approached her, but was afraid to touch her. She looked so sick to him, weak and frail. He folded his arms across his chest, holding in some body heat. It was damn cold in here, and she was sleeping nude on top of the covers, wrapped around one of his pillows. He waited while she stirred coming out of a deep sleep. His mind scrambled for something to say, some action to use to communicate all he was feeling.

The heat made Regina fight to wake up. The last thing she wanted to do is spend the rest of the night in the kitchen cooler. She hoped the air wasn't on the blink again. She rolled to her back, checking to make sure cool air blew from the vent over the door. She couldn't see the vent. She couldn't see the door. All she could see was Mitch. Commander Mitchell Bolton, deceased.

Closing her eyes with a tired sigh, Regina dropped her head back to the mattress.

"Oh, it's you again. Mitch, when will you leave me alone? I see you every day and you are carving my heart out."

He watched her close her hand around something on a chain around her neck.

"I love you and I will until I die. But I don't know how much longer I can survive seeing you appear and disappear in my life." Defeat filled her whispered words, barely heard over the wash of air from the fans trained to cool her.

Mitch moved to the bed and scooped her up into his arms. The quiet, ravaged sound of her voice shredded his heart, only now beginning to beat again. He settled with her in his lap, the way they used to cuddle. The Drakken keened, the strange mourning sound filling his head, spilling into his heart.

Regina stiffened against him and then relaxed. Her skin tingled where he touched her. For a moment fear kept her eyes closed and then the scent of warm Mitch flooded her head, opening her eyes. This was not a ghost appearing again to taunt and haunt her. She lifted a hand to touch him, but curled her fingers to her palm.

Mitch shook his head. Pulling her hand up to his lips, he kissed the white knuckles.

"Regina, I'm real. I almost died, but I escaped," he whispered to her. "I've come back for you."

"You can't, I can't leave here. The experiment changed me, made me so different. I can't leave this cold storage." Tears tracked down her face as she waved a hand to include the room. Overwhelmed, her emotions tangling inside, she didn't bother to wipe away the wet tracks.

"We are leaving together this time. I'm not leaving you here alone, not again," he assured her, his mind already searching for solutions. Mitch wondered how he could survive these temperatures with her here, and the enormous problem this presented with getting her through the desert, which reached temperatures in the day of one hundred plus degrees. He would work on that later, now he wanted to hear what had happened from Regina.

"What happened, after?" His voice shook. Suddenly he wasn't sure he wanted the details of her life after he'd taken the easy way out. He brushed her hair out of her face, wiping the tear tracks dry with his fingertip.

"After they took the rest of the bodies to the morgue, the mad scientist ordered cremation of all the remains, signed the certificates electronically and sendt them off to his keepers. He packed and took every scrap of information out of here with him and the rest of his team. It was just as you predicted. Once the elevator was topside we were locked out of using it. Trapped down here, we started helping each other, finding most of the other personnel had left with the majority of the techs, doctors." While there was exhaustion in her voice, there was no anger.

"The military sent word that funding would continue for those of us still here, understanding that we might never leave this facility. A small team of support personnel would stay to assist.

"Mike and Tracy chose to stay, Tracy because of her soldier, and I suspect that Mike and Hanover are in love. He hasn't said, but he's worked his ass off trying to find any forgotten information I can use to help them out. Help us out.

"I came down here to see what had happened, if all of you died. I hadn't heard anything and you didn't pop into the lab to make your notes." She lifted a hand, stroking the side of his face, clean-shaven and smooth.

"I'd checked my blood and wanted to let you know, for sure. Six men barely hanging on to their sanity met me, fresh from the showers. Some of them scrubbed the skin off their bodies. Tracy joined me with some animal tranqs and we put them under. In the hours that followed we pieced together some of what happened down here, but not all of it." She looked up at Mitch.

"The military can keep a secret, you know." She smiled a little. Mitch thought it looked like a grimace. He bet his team hadn't wanted to talk about it. With him gone and no firm direction to go, the men had banded together as survivors.

"Anyway, I started working with them, knowing the secret to getting them out would be to desensitize them to the light wavelength. I worked them under the light until they could keep rotating on the exercise machines without attempting to kill each other." She stirred, searching for a cool spot.

"You have to let me go, Mitch. You're too hot." Regina stretched off his lap and aligned her body to his, blocking him from the fan's breeze. When her body started cooling off she sighed with relief.

"So we worked the guys and we worked in the lab. We lived around the clock from day to day, wondering when they would decide to "cleanse" the base and using every second to find any answers. Mike found some information on an earlier study that sent us in a good direction for a solution. I don't know if it will cure us, but if I can get it there it will stop some of the progressions."

"What progressions?" Mitch had a feeling he already knew.

"Some of the men under stress will transform body parts. Their arms will become scaled and clawed. Or their head and neck will shift toward reptile, expanding their human hearing and increasing their reaction times in attack." She turned her head to look at him.

"Do you not have any adverse effects from the test?" Regina stiffened and sat up. She pulled away from him, grabbing and holding his pillow to her chest. "Did dying erase the effects in your system?" Suddenly she became animated.

He swallowed hard. Gazing at her, the pale skin showing a slight flush of color, her eyes bright in inquiry, he hated he had to dash the sudden hopefulness in her eyes. "No, dying is what finished the experiment."

Confusion replaced the hopefulness in a wave. "Dying finished it. How did dying help with that?"

"Not the dying part. I did not die. I was aware of everything that happened with me. I thought I reached for your hand in the corridor, but you touched me. I spoke to you, but you didn't hear me. I was alive when they locked me into the crematory oven to finish me."

Leftover horror washed through him. He controlled the emotion with deep breaths, only to lose the tentative grip when he looked up to find a matching expression on her face.

"Oh, Mitch," Regina murmured. . "If I had known…"

He shook his head, struggling to get the shudders under control.

"I know that, Regina. I've had time to be okay with it. After I escaped from here it took me some time to get straight in my head. I had the whole desert to play in. Then a little Buddhist monk adopted me. He worked me day and night to accept what happened to me, to help me get my head right, to work to find triggers and how to fight the aggression." He reached for her hand, pulling it from the grasp on the pillow.

"I changed like Miller did. I became a huge reptile with wings." He watched her. "I am a Drakken, if what Chin Yeo told me is right, and my other form is a great red dragon."

Chapter 21

Regina listened to him. Remnants of her dream, the one she shared with him the night before the end, floated out of her subconscious. The red dragon and the smaller blue dragon tied in a mating plummet. They shared the skies, powerful wings pulling them through the air. She pushed it away, searching for an answer in his explanation.

"You have accepted this?" Her mind ran through research currently working in the lab. "I think it may be permanent, Mitch. I can't get a virus to live long enough to make any changes to the affected DNA." She wondered if the DNA shift had attacked his mind, dragging him into some psychosis she didn't have a name for.

"Yeah, I've met the dragon and lived." He smiled, remembering the small monk strapped to his muscled back, cackling like a mad man while Mitch flew through the sky.

"Can I have some blood?" A growing excitement reinforced the healthier glow to her face.

He nodded, his gaze softening as he looked over her. If he wasn't sane, he wouldn't be here. She had to accept that. She had to accept he was here in the flesh, because if she didn't she was lost to the insanity of her condition. She carried the debilitating fear with her all the time.

"I'll give blood until it hurts if you'll eat with me." He watched her, aware of the problems her staff had with her diet. There had been comments from the team here. Even Tracy had mentioned her fragility.

A self-conscious glance down showed her body through his eyes. The bones in her knees looked like weapons, her muscles hanging off the tendons. No wonder he did not react to her body like before. That body was long gone. All that was left of her was her mind and the skeleton she kept alive in a cooler. She'd long ago stopped looking into a mirror, seeing her image in the eyes of her tech assistants.

She saw it in the glances from the surviving team members. Her clothes, never snugly fitted, hung off her until she lived in scrubs, the boxy cut of material hiding her true weight loss. She pulled the pillow between them again, hiding from his steady gaze. She was no longer the woman he'd taken to bed, the supple wanton who learned to ride his body in their shared pleasure.

She had forgotten that Mitch's psi talents included telepathy. It never crossed her mind at all, leaving her an open book to him. He heard every thought. He watched disgust start to cross her face before he reached for her. Pulling her back into his lap, he tossed the pillow from between them. He wrapped his hand in her hair, dull but still beautiful to him, and held her for his kiss, the kiss he dreamed of giving her, all his heart and soul, all his life to her. Under his skin, the Drakken growled, urging him to finish the claim. Energy pulsed against his flesh, warmth flooded him and Regina moaned into his mouth.

Regina burned, his skin roasting her until dizziness consumed her. If he had not held her so tightly she would have fallen. She needed to pull away, since her body was unaccustomed to the temperatures of his. The kiss was worth every minute of this hell she inhabited. Trying to find a cooler embrace, she moved over him.

Feeling her in his arms again brought the expected results. He rearranged her as his body searched for room to expand. Regina came to life under his touch. She moved until she straddled his thighs. Mitch thrust to meet her, feeling her heat deep from that cold body, cupping his cock through the pants separating them. Mitch kissed her until his head clouded. He needed this woman, now and forever.

The fighting was over. She was as much a victim as his handpicked men. He wondered why he'd ever doubted her, even as he'd taken the step to buy a ring to bind them. He'd been blind in his anger and panic. The Drakken had taken away his humanity while absorbing the life experiences through Mitch.

"Forgive me, Regina." She pulled back, her hands tangled in his hair, dragging the leather tie binding it free.

"What for?"

"I doubted you for so long. I blamed you for the trouble we were in, for the experiment. I didn't confess to you soon enough—"

Her hand slipped over his mouth. She panted, her breath warm now with her arousal puffed in little clouds from her parted, reddened lips.

"It's over. I forgave you long ago. You came back. For whatever reason, you're here now. Let's start this over." She teased him with her lips, watching him as she kissed him, tugging his lower lip between hers until he cradled her head in his palm and took control.

The fragile hold Regina kept on her calm and sanity slipped away. The animal part of her brain, the one she half lived in since the transition, took hold. She arched and pulled him to her. Her body writhed against his, thrusting and moaning in frustration when she could not get what she wanted, needed. Her hold on Mitch became grasping, her body struggled against his in extreme agitation, and tears streaked her face, bathing his in the wetness.

Inside, dormant, her dragon woke. Sensing her mate close, she rushed forward, bringing Regina with her. The woman and the dragon tangled, reaching for the one, their male. Strength she'd forgotten filled her, the dragon potent now she had her mate beside her.

Mitch pulled her off him, shaking her to stop the gasping, mewling cries from her throat. Her mind was foreign to him, yet the same. He felt the animal, recognized it, but then emotions swamped the tentative identification. Looking down at her in his arms, writhing with need and something he couldn't name, he gasped.

Blue eyes opened, not with round pupils, but long ones. Under her skin, the cold flesh rippled and blue scales rose against it, imprinting the pattern there. Inside Mitch, his dragon growled, curling protectively toward his mate, need rising to the surface. Mitch put the Drakken in its place. Regina needed him more.

"Regina, come back to me." He tried to talk her down. With his voice and with his mind linked to hers, he coaxed her, commanded her.

She fought him, afraid to let him go, afraid he would disappear and leave her to be the strong one alone.

He should have realized that everyone down here looked to her for leadership. She'd been strong for everyone, keeping her doubts and fears secret. There was no one to whom she could turn, letting them take the load from her. The yoke of command embedded into her flesh and bone she couldn't release to anyone.

It should have been no surprise. In a life or death situation, someone had to step up and stop the madness. There had been one person so deeply involved, so tied to the last team, their nemesis and their savior. The weight was too much for one inexperienced, fragile woman to carry.

"Regina, I'm here and I am not going anywhere. You can lean on me now."

Mitch lost count of the times he assured her before her body relaxed in his arms. Hiccups from the crying still stuttered through her, tears and sweat bathed her body from the emotional release and being next to his body. She did not have the strength left to jump when her doorbell rang. Mitch eased her back to the bed, crawling over her to answer the summons. Tracy and Conway were standing there. He could hear Manny in the corridor.

"Is she—" Tracy nodded toward Regina's room.

"Check on her, tell her I have to…" Mitch watched as Tracy nodded and slipped by him as he headed out.

He stood in the corridor for a moment, letting his body warm up, working his hands into fists to pump warm blood to his extremities. Would her dragon always need this coldness to survive? Would she be able to fully shift forms and become the reptile? He had more questions than answers and he needed all of them free of this facility before it was pounded into rubble over their heads.

His feet were cold in his boots and he wondered how they were going to fix this between them. The murmur reminded him duty called and no one had a way to stop the clock. Conway stayed with him as he moved to see how Manny and Trevor were doing.

"Let us see what Mitch thinks about it first, is all I'm saying." Trevor was trying to placate Manny.

From the tone of her voice, she was having none of it.

"What does Mitch have to think about now?" he asked, rounding the corner and finding his team standing there.

Manny and Trevor looked at each other then at him. He crossed his arms over his chest, looking mildly from one to the other. He managed to put everything in his mind to rest. Later he would have time to explore and fix things between Regina and him. He'd seen her for himself, held her close to his heart. It wasn't the wine and roses moment he'd dreamed about, but it was a hell of a lot closer than he had an hour ago.

Manny shuffled her feet and then locked him with her gaze. "A thought." She held up a hand fist tight, one finger upright. "When the elevator starts to move, the upper levels receive warning something is happening. If we don't use explosives, you know I hate that, but no big bangs. We can use Trevor's arrows, strung to release when the door opens. He has a ninety-nine percent kill rate with his goodies, but it won't injure all and sundry at the door." She looked at Trevor. "We have to assume that level techs and civilians might work and live on separate floors and need the transport. Of course, that presupposes that the raiders will let them go between work and home."

"Boss, I can rig them to shoot on—"

"No, can't risk it." He cut Trevor off, something he rarely did with any of his team. Mitch didn't realize he was already shaking his head. "Trevor, you are the crack shot with them, it would be easier to let you be in the box ready to shoot when the doors open." He realized then that he played right into Trevor's argument.

Manny was shaking her head now.

"Won't work, there is no place he can hide from auto weapons fire." Manny smirked back at Trevor.

"That's not necessarily true." Forgotten as he stood behind Mitch, Conway spoke up. All eyes turned to him.

"We have metal sheets made of the same thing as tank armor. All we need to do is take it up to the next floor, fashion a blind, and put him in it." Conway looked at the three of them. "Set him up in a duck blind, kinda." He shrugged.

Mitch studied him. He could see how it would work. Manny shook her head. Trevor looked like a bobble head doll his chin did so much bouncing. Mitch sighed. He glanced at his watch, they had less than six hours.

"Okay, let us check in with Ben, Williams and Moody. They may have help for us." Mitch started in the direction of the gym. His boots ringing in the hall, finally his feet were warming up. His heart ached for Regina, but he would work on that problem. He was not leaving her behind, not again. He hoped it wouldn't kill her to get her free.

The shop rang with hammers and the hiss and sparkle of welding. A blind took shape, cobbled together of enough metal to keep Trevor safe and to be light enough to carry to the elevator.

Moody watched the raiders as morning started lighting the sky.

Ben dozed on the desk beside Moody. He'd circumvented many of the bio traps set to kill in the access tunnels. Probably the smartest of them, he was catching a nap when he wasn't needed. The others were starting to flag.

Their level was empty except for Tracy, Mike and Regina. All of whom were currently in the lab working with Mitch's blood. With Hanover and Carlisle escorting the last group of civilians out, with orders to stay and protect them, they were down to a skeleton crew. His team and Conway, Williams, Adams and Moody stayed *Below*. Luckily, they hadn't triggered any systems topside that would alert the remaining raiders to what was happening through the access passages. Taking only what they needed, the civilians followed the soldiers up and out, escaping *Below* and waiting for rescue.

The next level would need stealth and blessings. Mitch teamed Conway and Williams with Manny and set Adams and Moody with him. Ben would watch and communicate with them via the ear buds everyone wore. Trevor was in the blind to flush out the bad guys and kill them.

Jake used their isolated system to call in pickup for the facility personnel along with monitoring the time line and the whole facility spy system. Luckily for them, the little cameras so well hidden in the shadows had escaped the notice of the raiders. They had not started shooting them out or disabling them.

Mitch, Conway and Williams were collecting the facility personnel and sending them up the tunnels with Hanover and Carlisle. The stitches didn't encumber Hanover, they would probably add another interesting story while picking up women, and Carlisle's concussion was much better, only hours after receiving it.

"Something to do with the starfish, Doc Reggie told us. Bad injuries heal a little quicker. Little injuries heal in no time." Clearly, the twenty-two year old had a crush on Doc Reggie. Mitch could hear it in his voice, see it in the slight blush on his face. He hoped Carlisle wouldn't be devastated when Regina came with Mitch.

There were a lot of miles between hope and dreams, and Mitch wanted everyone out of here, yesterday. There was a lot of work hanging between danger and security.

"Boss, we have ground support at five miles. Air support confirms no bogies in or around the area. Raider force must be awaiting contact for extraction."

"Send directions to Hanover and Carlisle, let ground know to expect them."

Mitch followed the next fifty or so civilians through the house to

Carlisle. The rest of his team was sweeping level five. Manny's team was on four, the more dangerous because that is where the true base functions operated. He waited every minute for explosions, but so far Manny had not loosed any mass destruction. Mitch knew his luck could not hold out. It was only a matter of time.

"Boss, level five is clear. Continuing up to meet and sweep with team one."

"Roger. Anyone coming up?"

"Negative, you have all the lost sheep."

"Roger."

Time he headed *Below*. He wanted Regina out with him, her safety foremost in his mind and heart. The two organs seemed to have reached an accord while he worked to empty the base of personnel.

He hefted the rifle, his right hand in situations like this, and turned back. A crack sent him out the door of the ranch and into the desert. Someone was taking shots at the topside team. Thankful he had on his desert cap and BDUs that blended him with the scenery, he settled in to find the shooter.

"Carlisle?"

"Roger that."

"Did you see where?"

"Shooter is in the Northwest corner, on a rise behind the house. We're in a ditch, all safe."

Mitch reversed direction, headed to the back of the house.

"Boss, the sniper is at your one o'clock." *Thank you, Jake.* Mitch turned toward the area reported. He watched, hoping to see a reflective flash since it was so early in the morning. He wrapped the sling around his arm, focusing through the scope, scanning the area.

There, he watched the sun strike a reflection on the glass eye of a scope. He followed the barrel back. Shit, he clearly saw the tripod. This meant their sniper hid with no liabilities. He could not shoot out his hand or arm. The shooter remained safe behind the rifle. Mitch moved into the yard, almost due west, hoping to flank him. Another shot rang into the morning before Mitch found a vantage point.

"Carlisle?"

"One casualty, civilian."

Mitch counted three raiders in the burrow. Good place to be if you weren't dealing with a professional. Mitch prioritized his shots, settled himself and took the raiders out, one, two and three.

"Move out carefully. This bunch is gone, but there is no guarantee that others aren't around."

"Will do, Boss."

Mitch moved into the burrow, toeing the bodies over to check them. Their radio crackled and he turned it off. Nothing other than some rations, water and ammunition survived. Mitch dismantled the rifle and took everything with him. He loaded the backpack with rations and settled the weight on his back. He started out of the burrow.

"Boss, back into the hole." Jake's voice broke into his thoughts. "You have three, again three raiders heading your way from the east."

Mitch dropped the pack and settled against the side of the burrow in the shade. He pulled his barrel back as far as it would go, hoping the rising sun would not give him away. He listened to the desert start to sigh as the sun warmed up the sand.

"Boss, you have three more raiders heading your way. Total six raiders coming to you."

The voice was emotionless, but the rush of adrenalin was anything but.

Mitch felt the aggression swell in his system. His hard won control battled with the knowledge of killers on his six. The double heartbeat quickened, his body stretching to change. He stilled the movements, considering his options. Quickly Mitch discovered he had no options. Sliding in the shade, he pulled out of his clothes and boots. Desert heat fed his body. He changed forms and exploded out of the hole as dragon kin.

Chapter 22

Taking to the skies, he scouted the moving silhouettes. Winging into the sun, he shifted to his large form between one wing beat and the next. He followed the shadow of his wings back to the desert floor, roaring fire onto the first bunch of three. He barely heard their screams. Heavier now some of his lift was gone, he searched for another source. Chin Yeo made sure he could find the elements he needed. Eyes peeled to the desert floor, he heard Ben in his head.

"Go back toward the bodies, behind the wash is a rock slide. You will find what you need there." Mitch banked and headed toward the black smoke.

"Thanks." Sure enough, he scooped up the elements, chewing while his lift bladders filled up. That witch knew everything and Mitch was thankful. Without the earpiece, he couldn't communicate normally. He had to rely on the mental link with Ben. Or not. He chewed another mouthful of the powdered materials. Experimenting, he reached for Jake, telepathically.

"Jake, can you hear me?"

"Boss, if that's you, you have three on the other side of that wash." Jake's voice was not so steady.

Mitch was fine with that. It was a shock to them, this change of their CO. He enjoyed the wash of brain chemicals in his body along with the digestion of fuel lifting him on heavy wings for another run. He swept the top of the wash with his tail, sending loose scree and gravel over the raiders. While they ducked he gained altitude.

"Jake, are there any others out here that you spotted?"

"No bogies moving at this time. The last three have split up and are circling with weapons trained on you." While Jake adjusted, he spoke to Mitch aloud from his end, but Mitch heard the echo in his mind. Sharply focused, Jake used everything he knew to get through to Mitch.

Mitch found them, wondering if bullets would kill him in this form. He'd never been shot at, though Chin Yeo used to throw rocks at him. That happened mostly when the little monk was angry, or to get Mitch's attention when it wandered.

Mitch swept in low, taking out two of them, one with a small blast of fire, one with his talons. That left him with one. He circled, dropping the dripping mess of the raider. Another low dive with the sun at his back, he ripped the last one in two. Sweeping high into the sky, he saw the group heading for transport. He flew in growing circles, scouting the area carefully before returning to the burrow and dressing.

"*Mitch, you need to be down here.*" The terse statement came from Ben to his mind.

He ran the distance to the ranch, dropping through the air duct. It was smaller and faster if he rode down it like a slide. He ignored the rips in his clothes and his flesh, taking the flat levels at speed, sliding between floors to reach the morgue and then the bottom level.

"*Ben, what's up? I'm between floors heading down.*"

"*Mitch, we need you in the kitchen, the freezer.*" Mitch felt the power in the witch now. He burst through the air cover, hitting the ground running for the dining room.

"*Where is the freezer?*" He stopped in the dining room, breathing hard, the taste of sulfur in his sinuses burning. He waited for an answer when Ben appeared through a swinging door.

"Come on, man. I don't know how much longer we can hold her." Ben disappeared back through the door.

"What do you mean, hold her?" he shouted as he leaped the counter and stiff-armed the door, right on Ben's heels. The sight that met him stopped his advance, filling him with panic. Writhing on the floor, her body twisting in unimagined pain, Regina moaned in strangled pants. He rushed into the twenty-degree box, barely registering the door closing behind him. He pulled Regina off the floor, his mind reaching for Ben, even though they were now side-by-side with the insulated aluminum of the freezer door between them.

"*What happened?*" His jaw clenched so tightly he couldn't utter a word.

"She was in the lab, working on whatever she was doing. After she synthesized your blood, Tracy was too slow to stop her from injecting herself. She did manage to pull Regina's blood before her body locked up. Tracy is studying it now, with Mike. Regina needed to chill quickly, so we brought her here, settling her on the floor, the coolest part of the box.

"She started convulsions soon after her core dropped in temperature below seventy degrees." Ben sighed on the other side of the door Mitch could feel his frustration. Without the full knowledge of everything their bodies underwent, Ben had nothing to work with. When Mitch brushed the hair off Regina's face, her body calmed down. He could not get into her mind. It was shut against from him every way.

He shivered, especially after being in the hot sun. Ben opened the door and threw him a parka. How the man found one on this desert base Mitch had no idea.

"So, don't ask. I don't think this guy will miss his for a few." Ben laughed. Mitch shrugged into the coat, pulling it closed around his body. The fans were busy lowering the wind chill on them from twenty degrees to below zero. Regina was calming as the temperature dropped.

"Mitch?" Ben was following a line of thought. He'd been filtering through Mitch's mind, open now with the emotional currents leaving his thoughts and memories exposed.

"Yeah?" Mitch pulled a pallet under his ass. He would be damned if he would sit on that cold metal. It was bad enough Regina was comfortable there. He raised her shoulders to rest her head in his lap, keeping his heat a little farther from her but needing the contact to keep his Drakken under control.

"You got this, too, right? That's how you ended up where you are." Ben was being careful, picking his words with care.

"Yes, I was here when the mad scientist infected us. I was in the last group with the six guys still here. Regina was tricked into taking the same serum injections as the only female down here available." Mitch pulled the hood up as Regina finally uncurled in his arms. She sighed in comfort.

"How did you manage…?"

"I slipped into catatonia, the doctor ordered me put in a crematory oven. While I was locked in there, the fire cured the imbalance in my system without killing me." His mind flooded with details he remembered but had forgotten before now.

Ben was there, following his train of thought, making long leaps in logic. Even Chin Yeo was part. He remembered the little monk teaching him about dragons. The heat, cold, water, earth all kept their guardians as dragons among the other forms. It dawned slowly on Mitch.

"Ben—"

"I'm already there, Boss. I'll be with you in a sec." Mitch sensed movement outside then silence. Ben was gone. Mitch opened the scrubs Regina wore with his knife, splitting the fabric and folding the material away from her body. For modesty's sake, he folded the fabric over her hips, her breasts he left bare. Beneath those taut nipples, her heart and lungs struggled to keep her alive. He wanted to give her every chance to survive, and if that meant incasing her organs in ice, he was all for it. The thought of all that freezing air covering her body made him shiver, but she stretched as though she enjoyed the frozen kiss.

The door opened on Ben, who held a medical kit in his hand. Wrapped in another parka, he joined Mitch on the pallet looking at Regina.

"Tracy told me if we have to, to inject her with this." He held up the kit. "If we don't need it don't use it."

"How will we know?" Mitch asked. He hated riddles.

Ben shrugged.

Mitch felt Ben pull a powerful shield around them in the cold. He didn't see anything but felt if he reached out a hand he would contact a thick wall enclosing them. He didn't know how Ben did it, but there had been other times when the witch had done something they didn't understand that had saved their asses more than once.

"I will need your strength to summon the *ones who slumber*." Ben told him, the last three words emphasized and cryptic. Mitch nodded, taking a deep breath and exhaling fog. He'd do anything to save her. Mitch felt other minds joining them outside. Moody and then Williams joined Tracy and Jimmy Adams.

"John and Max, I need you in the freezer!" Ben shouted through the door. The door opened and the two men stepped inside. Ben was already opening the circle to include the others, his mental explanation bringing them up to speed.

Moody looked everywhere except at Regina on the floor, Williams hunkered down beside Ben as if he'd always worked with them. Both of the men had good telepathy scores, which would definitely help.

Ben closed the circle behind them then resettled beside Mitch and

Regina.

"You know what's happening, right?" Mitch nodded. Regina, against all odds, was becoming the blue dragon. Her dream, his dream resurfaced. Together they had flown, locked in a mating flight. She would be smaller than he was, her scales made of countless shades of blue and green. Her Drakken would be born in ice, complimenting his birth in fire.

He looked down at her in his arms. If she survived, she would undergo the same birth in her element that he did for his. A glance at the two others assured him that a force of Drakkens huddled inside the magick circle. Chin Yeo talked of these dragons, shifters that were born to do so, huge guardians of the history and the magick that controlled their kind.

Ben reached into the shadowed chaos of Regina's mind. He found the flame within her, the spark that was keeping her alive, her all-consuming love for Mitch. He coaxed it brighter, blocking thoughts that were harmful to his working.

Mitch leaned in with him, pouring his love back to her, feeding her his strength.

Max Williams placed his hands on the floor, reaching for a connection, some experience showed in the smile he sent Ben.

John Moody drifted around the circle, not touching the walls. He couldn't settle down, didn't want to see his Doc Reggie in such bad condition. Whips of anger flailed him from Mitch and Ben. He thrust those thoughts from his head, standing with his back ramrod straight, facing the door. He allowed Ben to take from him, pulling him into the greater working whole.

Together Ben wove the energies around Regina, waking her to her place in the guard. He focused his power on the elements, earth, air, fire and water. He pulled strength from the enhanced men, directing it to the cold cocoon around Regina. He had to get her below zero before the dragon would emerge. He did not know how he knew this. He simply accepted that it was so.

Mitch watched as Max settled further toward the floor, more of his big body touching the freezing metal. He watched as frost formed on Regina's body. Her skin turned blue as her body pulled blood to her vital organs. In time her brain would shut down, she would die. Mitch shifted his thoughts to her survival, their love. Fear tried to crowd inside, his or one of the others he did not know, but he banished it with the aid of the strength of his Drakken.

"Great guardians of the North, East, South and West, hear us in our time of need. Join us in our circle. Send us your strength and guidance. We hold four of your great beasts here, one struggling for birth.

"One consumed by the flame of the South answered your call.

"The second is claimed by the ice of the West, she is frail, her body too weak. We need your strength to hold her soul with us. She is not the guardian of the dance of water, but comes from your demesne.

"Aided by the guardian spirit of the North whose body bridges the power of the earth to the power of our Great Mother.

"We are aided by the guardian spirit of the East whose body aids the winds generated around the fallen guardian." Ben paused for a moment.

Mitch felt the circle thicken, the wind picked up as Moody started fidgeting again. Williams grunted with strain and Mitch felt heat begin to radiate. He worked to shut off the rise.

"Great Lord and Lady, we have four of your chosen children together, working for each other. Even though there are your children, they were unprepared for your calling. Help the mortal bodies survive their transition. If it is your desire, allow these to be together, fire and ice.

"Also, aid the Air and the Earth to enter your guard. We petition you this day when our time is short." Ben watched hoarfrost coat the woman, her breaths coming only four to five times a minute. She was nearly dead. If divine intervention didn't happen soon, he didn't know if he could bring her back.

Suddenly Moody turned and put both hands on Regina's legs.

From this touch, Ben and Mitch watched as a white cloud enveloped her body. Regina bowed off the floor then dropped boneless back to her position. Mitch stared, knowing she was dead. Shock held him immobile. Before he could roar his fury and grief, Max wrapped an arm around his waist. Immediately Mitch felt strength and reassurance flood his body. He poured what he could into his link with Ben and Regina.

"We thank you, Great Ones, for attending us in our time of need. We thank you for answering our pleas. We thank you for guarding us in this time outside of time. Congratulations on the birth of your new sentinels." Ben sat back, reaching a hand to Max. Mitch felt the bubble collapse around them.

When Moody headed for the door, the latch opened before he touched it. He glanced over his shoulder at Ben who shrugged.

Mitch heard snippets of conversation between them, but didn't pay too much attention. Max was an extremely joyous force between Mitch's shoulder blades. He stood up, shivering in the cold and reached to shake Ben's hand before he followed Moody out.

Ben stood last, watching the cloud over Regina undulate in a breeze of its own making. He found the flame, strong and steady. He led Mitch there, feeling him take over the nurturing of her soul. He shut the door, leaving the two of them alone.

Mitch let more of his heat through. He was shivering a little too much. His feet again were freezing. He couldn't resist picking her up in his arms. Her body settled against him, no weight to her at all.

"Mitch?" Her voice a mere whisper of air.

"Regina, I'm here." He told himself to ignore the welling of his eyes. The image of ice cubes rolling down his face helped.

Regina shuddered in the cold. It had been a long time since she felt anything but warm. Now she needed to warm up, quickly. The cold she'd craved for months now hurt her.

Mitch caught her thought and upped his body heat. He pulled off his parka and wrapped Regina in the warm interior. He left the remains of her scrubs on the floor and carried her out of the cold.

The applause startled them. Tracy claimed the kit from his hand, tucking it behind her back. She smiled and left them to return to the lab. In the dining room, someone had taken the time to set out a buffet. It wasn't fancy, but it would work.

"Jake, how is our time?" Mitch felt out of touch. He knew they'd been in the freezer for an hour or more. He was that tired. With the touch of exhaustion, he was beginning to feel the hold on his libido and his dragon slipping.

"We are heading into our fifth hour down and counting. There is no further movement upstairs, no communication in or out. Our sheep are loaded and leaving. Our shepherds are sneaking back to the fold. We are in need of caffeine and food, hint-hint." Jake laughed.

"Take a break and join us down here. We have a buffet to tackle." Mitch pulled the team together. "You guys go ahead and eat. We'll be right back." He carried Regina back to her quarters.

Carol Shaughnessy

Chapter 23

The door opened into another refrigerator. Regina shivered in his arms. Rich, warm blood flushed her cheeks, returning her to a closer to normal color. He lowered her to the floor, watching in amusement as her toes curled away from the cold.

"Can we get some heat in here?" Regina pulled the parka closer around her, trying to shut out the air gaps.

"Are you sure, you told me you needed this." Mitch walked past her, adjusting the thermostat to turn off the cold and start warming up the apartment.

"Yeah." Regina nodded. She could feel the difference in her body. Being reborn seemed to have reset her internal thermostat. It should allow her to keep regular temperature settings now. She wanted to study the change, take blood, and examine it for other clues. She needed to start the research into all of this.

"Yeah, I can go back to normal," she told him in growing assurance and no small surprise at the discovery. She smiled at Mitch, wanting to jump back into his arms. Her libido warmed with a welcome sinuous stretch of the creature under her skin. She realized then the dragon inside of her was real and doing everything in her power to strengthen her for her mating.

Mitch opened the door and propped it so it couldn't close. The wash of cold air filled the corridor and dispersed. Regina checked the set of her thermostat. Mitch had it at seventy-eight. As soon as the ambient temperature rose, it would be comfortable here. She went into the bathroom and started the water. She felt sticky, wet, and needed to wash off the past and the freezer floor.

Stepping under the warm water, she smiled. Almost back to normal, she found herself repeating the same heart filled thank-you to the universe. A voice interrupted her chorus with a faintly mocking, *"You're welcome."*

She smiled back at Ben, and then chuckled as Mitch cut him off. She was still laughing when he stepped into the shower with her. His hands slipped over her body, catching the bubbles from her shampoo. His warmth surrounded her, heating her mind along with her body. Slippery, she turned in his arms, wrapping around him.

Mitch pulled her slick, warm body against his. He'd returned for this woman, this feeling, this warmth, this part of his heart. The incredible seesaw of his mental state settled, the missing piece of his life was here in his arms. For once, even his Drakken was quiet, reveling in her closeness. Regina arched her body into his, soaking in the water and his heat.

His body responded predictably. His cock nudged the soft skin of her belly as if he needed any encouragement. He kissed her, pulling her hair back, arching her neck for his mouth. He licked the soft skin of her shoulder, and then struck into her neck with his teeth. He left his mark on her skin. When he pulled back and saw her reddened flesh, he enjoyed the satisfaction of knowing she belonged to him. Regina sighed, gray eyes closed in pleasure.

"More." Her voice was rough, and he paused to study her. She'd been through hell the last hour, the last day, hell every day since he'd escaped, facing life as a Drakken without a mate.

He lifted her body, turning them. His hands cupped her ass as Regina locked her legs around his back. He lowered her body, finding the warm center. His shaft nudged past the oval entrance slick with soap and her own honey and moved inside her. Regina bucked against him, forcing him deeper into her body. His body clenched in the first of his orgasms, a gift from the dragons. He held her still, relishing the pulsing warming heat of her body on his. He stretched her fully, then he moved, beginning the ride for her again, bringing her along with him this time.

"I hope this doesn't become a habit." Her Drakken laced her voice with a noticeable growl.

"What?" He grunted, grinding his hips into hers. His brain was half-aware as he relished the feel of her around him. He'd staked his claim and instinct began to take over.

"That you fuck me once every six months. Then disappear from my life." She bowed as her first orgasm shook her body. He felt her claws slide down his back, catching his flesh and leaving welted proof of her enjoyment. Her growl woke his Drakken. The male's deep strokes forced valuable nutrients into her, helping her body soak up the essence of their nature.

He bucked into her harder, pummeling his body against hers. Pulling back, he filled her again, jolted against her, abrading her back with the shower wall. He gave up trying to hold them both upright in the shower. With a sudden turn, he settled to his knees holding her with one arm until he stretched her out on the floor of the shower.

Now he could concentrate on bringing her pleasure. The first couple of orgasms cleared his mind from the fog of sex. He pulled her legs up, catching her behind the knees and opening her for his thrusts. The shower water beat a warm tattoo over them, mingling with the sounds of two people finding pleasure.

They moved to the bed, their bodies heated by the water and the activity. Skin damp and slick, Regina rubbed against him. "I need more." Hell, they both needed more. More than they had time to indulge.

Mitch's hand fell to her hip.

"Turn over." His voice didn't sound like his. He pulled away, leaving her grasping cunt empty of his cock while he helped her turn. He went to his knees. One big hand on her hip, the other wrapped around his cock, slick and shiny with her cream.

Regina responded, getting to her hands and knees. He moved in close behind her, and then thrust home in a powerful stab. Her body stretched, holding the length and girth with a grasp that took his breath. She arched, shuddered, her lips parted to breathe or beg for more, when his hand tangled in her hair, dragging her head up.

It didn't hurt, but it did kick her already raging libido into overdrive. A harsh cry slipped up her throat, filling the room. Her Drakken-self stretched under her skin, undulating as she accepted every drop of strength he imparted.

"Glad you like that." She couldn't nod agreement not as his cock stroked inside her, farther than ever. He was a possessed lover, guiding her along a path she never expected existed.

"I need more, Regina. Give me all of you." He growled in her ear, his body curved over hers as he worked his cock deep.

She would have bruises where the blunt, flared head contacted her cervix. She didn't care. The pain morphed into pleasure and vitality more incredible than she'd believed could happen, but she was experiencing it. She was reborn, newly made and mated to the strong male she'd needed to bring her from the brink of certain death.

He reared back, keeping one hand in her hair, using the other to pick up her leg, opening her impossibly for the stretch of his shuttling cock. The combination derailed her mind.

Regina became a creature of feeling, starving for more. The hand in her hair sent chills over her, tightening her nipples until the sensation needed to be assuaged. She lifted her hand, somehow maintaining her balance to pinch and roll the uber sensitive tip.

Another gasp worked through her lips. Behind her, he moved his hand to where she was most open. Unerringly he found her throbbing clit, distended from the little stretched hood. In a few devastating touches, he had her bowed and screaming, lost in a maelstrom of erotic, primal explosions.

Unable to come down from the high, she trembled in his hold. He eased the pace, lowering her leg and releasing his hold on her hair. Holding her as she trembled, he was not able to still completely for her to catch her breath.

"Regina, goddess." Breathy words delivered as he straightened behind her, giving his lungs and heartbeat time to recover. He looked down the length of her back, lightly sheened in sweat as they worked for satisfaction, for complete satiation.

Next to his belly, bare as he parted her curved cheeks, the little rosette tightened at his next thrust then eased. Powerless to resist the air kiss, he slicked a finger with the cream frothed between them and coated the wrinkled flesh. Another ember lit and he couldn't wait to breach the tightly held opening. His Drakken roared his dominance, his screeched claim of his mate. She would belong to him totally. The Drakken demanded the inescapable memory of her submission to him, to his beast, and to this final taboo.

He would make sure she'd enjoy every second of his dark possession. So much that she'd crave those feelings only he could give her. He teased and rubbed the opening, coating the flesh surrounding it until everything glistened. The tip of his finger nearly slipped past the first guardian ring.

In his arms Regina stilled and moaned, thrusting back to his body, keeping his cock busy stroking her cunt, soaking in the slickness leaking from him and from herself.

"I'm going to have you here." He pushed against the channel opening, letting it give as she could accommodate. He took possession of the barest inch, catching his breath as her body gave to pressure. The internal temperature warm, the muscles grasped around his finger, trying to drag him deeper.

Regina froze at the intrusion, her back stiffening.

He bared his teeth as she fought a moment.

Fighting to get away from the intensity of the pleasure waking in her, she experienced more pleasure than she'd ever imagined she could. She refused to give him the satisfaction of allowing him that entrance.

"You can't stop me, Regina. You belong to me." Somewhere he knew that. There would never be another like her. This slender doctor completed him in ways he had yet to discover. He would have all of her.

He slipped his finger deeper, letting her body ease at the penetration of a slick digit. Under him she squirmed as much as their position allowed.

Regina had no words and then her mind expanded. As if a wall fell between them, she knew he was inside her mind as well as her body. The sure knowledge, the intense security of that knowledge, threw her into a vortex of neon sounds, tastes and scents, she reeled with the surge of Mitch as he filled her mind, pushing all else away for now.

The constant in her chaotic world remained Mitch. His hold on her, surrounded her, claimed her as primal as that sounded, and she couldn't argue. His body filled hers and she did belong to this man, heart and soul.

"Yes, touch me, take me." It made sense in her head, but her mouth and tongue changed the root feelings, the emotional plea an offshoot of the litany running through her brain. She bucked against him, going up on her toes, lifting to him, inviting the pinching pain of his illicit intrusion.

"I need more, Mitch."

"I know, Regina. Hang on a bit longer. Let me guide you." His mind meshed with hers. She'd nearly overwhelmed his long studied control. His warmth filled her, the sexual tension strung through her so tight she neared a breaking point she feared to approach.

"I'll catch you. Know that, Regina. I'll always be there to catch you."

He pulled his finger free of the furnace hot clutch of her muscles, reaching for the tube of gel, forgotten by the bed. Snapping the lid open, he squirted the cool gel above the slightly stretched opening, letting her body heat soften and take the chill from it.

He returned, easing the slickness deeper into her, dragging a soft grunt from her, as she couldn't stop the deeper breach of her passage. He watched her flesh, the pale warming to peach tones, then as she gave him control, blue green scales ghosted under the thin layer.

Her body froze as sensations bombarded an already overwhelmed mind. Electrical impulses ricocheted from mind to body, sensitizing every inch of flesh. Could survive much more? Her womb ached, Her breasts throbbed in pleasured pain. Shudders raked her. She looked over her shoulder at him, her eyes taking on a soft radiance in the light of the bathroom fixture.

"You are so beautiful." In the center of the storm he paused, taking her in as a whole gift to him.

"Finish me, I'm dying. I can't breathe, can't move. Help me, Mitch." But not one word passed between them.

"Ssh, I'll take care of you."

She fought everything for a precious moment, fought the insane pleasure, the edge riding pain, the needs screaming for an answer shredding her entire being. Under the seething of mind, emotion and body, love bloomed and the surety of that had her relaxing under his dominating hands,

"I'm yours." It wasn't a regret or surrender. It was a declaration of strength and acknowledgement of her power. Dropping her head to clasped hands, she gave her trust to the one man who deserved everything. Her Drakken purred, giving everything and taking the strength from him, a fountain of youth and energy she sorely needed.

Mitch pushed aside everything but her passion. He resumed the long, easy thrusts. Better, in control as their minds synchronized. Gentling her, he then raised the needs between them again.

Her breath hitched, a shiver ghosted over her as his finger worked deep and began a counter thrust to his cock she couldn't hope to match. She tensed when he added another finger, two stretching her into another level of pleasure burning up her spine. Her mind loose in a galaxy of pleasure she'd never experienced before or ever hoped to explore. Heat engulfed her from head to toes. Her body jetted through multitudes of orgasms as the burn became so erotic her breath froze in her lungs.

"Let go, lover. Let me have it all." His voice, close to her ear, so loved in the near silence of the room led her to the edge.

There was no bottom. The sensations Mitch woke in her body were a heaving sea at her feet. Deeper his fingers thrust, tightening her rear channel, the thin barrier between his cock and fingertips full of nerves. All of them misfiring as fingers and cock glided past each other.

"Mitch," she gasped and then she fell over the edge, floating in an orgasmic world they created between them. Hard shudders racked her, the sensation of falling all too real as everything around her exploded turning her body inside out.

"Mitch." She thought she whispered, but maybe she'd screamed his name. Above her, behind her his roar filled her head, the noise echoed through her apartment before fading. Together at last, their dragons reached for each other, primal animals needing to mate as their human bodies locked in pleasure.

Regina faded with it, her body and mind unable to process the surfeit of pleasure, closing down.

Mitch knew the second she left him. Her touch in his mind closed off as she faded from consciousness.

A second roar followed the first, the male animal's denial of loss. He rolled to her side slender body completely limp. It took a moment for him to find her, her body nearly curled into a fetal position. She needed time to recover. He assured himself and the rampant beast inside him, trumpeted his displeasure at the loss of his mate.

He staggered to his feet, hands and belly covered in their mixed fluids, the scent a rare perfume he savored. Going into the bath, the light too bright, he cleaned himself quickly. Getting a towel and dampening a rag for her, he returned to her side. She moaned as he parted her thighs, deftly cleaning her from front to back and patting the reddened swollen flesh dry. He tossed the towels to the floor, unable to resist his animal's need to have her close.

He pulled the covers over her and tugged her to his side. Heat enveloped them and a quick check into her mind assured him she was resting falling deeper asleep as she calmed and warmed.

Chapter 24

"*We saved you a plate.*" Ben sent to Mitch some time later. Mitch stirred beside Regina reluctant to wake her. Time was still the enemy. In less than an hour, the base would be empty and ready for claiming by the rightful owners or it would be a failed mission and the tunnels so deep under the desert floor a pulverized sinkhole.

"*We'll be right over. Give us a minute.*" With a sigh he pushed the longer red coils away from her face. Some color returned to her skin as she warmed up, now he needed to get a few more pounds built back onto her. He lowered his head, moving his lips across Regina's swollen mouth. He pulled back to watch her slowly wake. He wanted to be there every time to watch her eyes blink sleepily up at him, then change from ice to fire when she recognized him.

He watched her tongue swipe her own lips as though searching out his taste. He looked lower as she stretched under the comforter, her shoulders bare. He counted the places she wore his marks. Primitive they might be, he was proud of each one of them.

"We need to get some food. When we get extracted I don't know when your next meal will be." He rolled off the bed, reaching for his pants. "Besides, you could use a few calories." He glanced over his shoulder. "I know I can, especially after the exercise."

Regina smiled and agreed. Slipping from the bed, she grabbed another set of scrubs and dressed. She couldn't help the fit, they hung on her diminished frame. She stretched in the welcome warmth of her quarters. Her Drakken woke, uncurling with more strength, thanks to her feeding.

Her body was her own once more, thanks to everyone's help. She watched Mitch tie his boots, his lanky frame bent double. She noticed his thinner body. Together they would get it back together. She yawned then turned to hug Mitch. Her eyes changed as she gazed up at him, taking on her Drakken's features.

"You are so beautiful." He kissed her and when he pulled back his eyes matched hers.

Chapter 25

Joining the others in the cafeteria was a brief celebration. For Regina, it was an awakening, her coming to life. In many ways it was a birthday for her. She could feel the foreign yet comfortable weight of another being in her head. The dragon was there all the time, integrated with Regina now, not a shadow but a friend. It must be much like Mitch felt with his resident dragon. She didn't have time now to study this facet but promised herself soon she would explore it in its entirety.

She ate, and for the first time in a long time it was good, delicious, in fact. She ate a full plate of food. Then swallowed the real vitamins Tracy brought to her. She followed that with a quart of water her system had lacked forever.

Mitch followed up with his team or teams now, at another couple of tables. It looked like the commander was back in business, the business of search and rescue. Time was of the essence when they cleared the last dishes and got back on leaving the facility. Tracy, Mike and Regina went back to the labs to gather every bit of data collected over the months incarcerated *Below*. They made backups of backups and stashed some of the more telling information where no one would find it.

Regina would not abandon her brotherhood, her family here, to the government without keeping some of the vital information for her continued research. As far as she was concerned, the government might as well consider them all dead and leave them alone. If what she suspected was true, all of them would be capable of housing the reptilian Drakken form, taking the form as needed.

She wanted blood samples and an arena to test out her theory, but most of all she wanted to feel the sun on her face again.

The task kept her busy and out of the operations end of business. Mitch was free to concentrate on wiping out the invaders and capturing their scientists. With Jake back in communications and Ben packing the stuff out of the labs as the crew there readied it, his team was now eight strong.

There were two ways to get upstairs, and the terrorists were down two more men, with another two wounded. All Trevor managed to take out his share. *Better some than none*. Mitch sent Manny to reload her bag, as she would be temporarily closing some of the exit points behind them as they left. Mainly she was to cover the vents he used to get in and out before.

Trevor, with Carlisle, Hanover, Adams and Williams loaded back into the elevator to see how many more militants they could draw out. Hanover and Adams were strong telekinetically, so anyone lobbing their brand of bang into the elevator would be very surprised to find the load coming back to them.

Conway, Moody and Mitch moved through the tunnels with packs of retrievable items from the labs. Jake would get with Manny as the last two to leave the base.

Jake loaded the virus disk he'd brought into the system, setting traps with key words given him by Regina. Those words when accessed would wake the sleeping virus and start the digestion process. The system would still work with the DOD but it would not allow them to access, process, or copy to backup any of the information on this project. It was the only way Mitch knew the information would stay safe.

Then Jake and Manny would send Ben, Tracy, Mike and Regina before them into the vent and follow them to the surface, making sure to close the doors behind them. When all the plans were set, Mitch asked for any questions. Every gaze met his with strength and determination.

Trevor and the folks on the elevators were to track the visiting scientists for capture, and if anyone actually survived their exit, to bring them along. Their survival wasn't a priority since they'd picked the wrong team to back.

If this terrorist sect found the R&D facility, Mitch's directive included finding answers about who they were, whom they had on the inside, and on what inside department of the government. This alone would take them to the end of their allotted time, making sure everyone made it out alive. Wasting no time, Mitch set them all to their tasks.

He spent a moment with Regina. Taking the chain from inside her scrub top, he pulled it over her head. With a twist, he broke the chain holding the emerald. Taking the ring in his hand, he studied it, remembering his first sight of the glowing stone. Going to one knee, he clasped it between his fingers and picking up her left hand, he slid the ring to her first knuckle.

"Regina Gardner, will you be my wife?"

Regina nodded. She didn't have the words. She hoped he could see that. She watched his face as he slipped the ring down her finger, then closed her hand to a fist.

He looked up to her eyes, his own eyes full of love. Gently he placed a kiss on her knuckles.

"I don't want to lose you again. We have a lot to catch up on and a lot of living to do. I want you to be with me. There are other studies we need to look into to help my team." Mitch pulled her into his arms, covering her lips with his, softly as a sigh, gently as the touch of a breeze. He coaxed her to meet him, to play with lightness and happiness.

Regina responded to his invitation with interest. Up on her toes, she wrapped her hands in his hair, longer than ever and curling around his neck. She licked her way over his hair-roughened skin to his throat, where she left her own mark of possession blushed on skin. She stuck to him like a burr as he tried to pull away, twisting in her arms. Growling softly in his ear, she nibbled there, feeling the chill bumps cross his skin.

"I will be yours until the end of time," she whispered. When she pulled back her gaze met his hazel one. "Somehow, I think that will be a very long time." Her heart slowed, the double beat easing at his agreement.

"I hope so."

Epilogue

Regina gasped as she changed forms from her Drakken to human. Beside her Mitch landed with more finesse.

Mitch covered her as Jimmy Adams and Max Williams shifted forms, landing close enough to kick up humus from the forest floor. "Not bad, but you need a little more practice."

The Drakken Brotherhood consisted of every team member who survived *Below*. They gathered at his cabin, a safe and secure place to practice these maneuvers needed to understand the curse gifted to them by Laurel and Regina.

Their name was passed from Mitch's Drakken, as they recognized their kin when all appeared. They both worried Mitch about their missing brother. He'd resorted to contacting Ben when no other answer surfaced.

Moody refused to shift his form from human, but in hand-to-hand he didn't hesitate to change his hands and arms, giving him six extra inches of reach and a hide so tough knives didn't pierce through.

Carlisle had recovered from his concussion, but while the Drakken called to him, the connection remained damaged.

This afternoon Ben Dugan leaned against the porch waiting for them all to assemble to help.

Hanover, always the last one to give in, glide back to earth, and assume his human form, drifted down. He did not have two forms and his solitary change was the smallest Drakken in the Brotherhood.

Sleek and charcoal gray, Hanover looked more bat like than Drakken, but as research proved, he was every bit as reptilian as his larger brethren.

"I'm getting the hang of this." He smiled, catching the robe Mike tossed his way. They embraced. Hanover picked his slighter bodied partner up and swung him into a circle in sheer exuberance.

They'd been working on this for a month, and Mitch was pretty sure they were ready to assimilate into his current team on an "as needed" basis. The Brotherhood was still battling mental syndromes of varied titles, so the R&R was sorely needed.

A regular diet and their beloved Doc Reggie helped them every day. Today would tell them about their last member to shift, to see if the bridges between nerves and muscles were strong.

"It's official, all of you suck eggs, rotten eggs." Carlisle left the porch to be close to them all.

"Then so will you." Max chuckled. "As soon as you get your head out of your ass and make this happen."

"That's what we're here for, I believe." Ben stepped off the porch then, waving a hand, he projected the circle around the Drakkens. "If you'll all join me." He moved to the center of his circle. Max immediately joined him to the left and Mitch to the right.

Carlisle went to his knees. All of this had been planned, so everyone knew their places. Ben called again to the guardians, and power swelled inside the invisible bubble of protection as they lent their strength to him for Carlisle.

Ben moved deftly and with great finesse through Carlisle's mind, finding a darkened area in his prefrontal cortex. Damage lived there, a blockade in his neuron highway. With the help of the guardians, he chose a spot where the damage looked severe and worked the thread free. Once he'd shown the powers around them what was needed, they took over, removing and repairing damage to his brain in an instant.

Carlisle fainted at the healing rush of heat.

"Don't break the circle. Regina, you can go to him in a second, they're almost finished." Ben told them, his eyes closed and his hands still out to his sides. He watched as every dark fiber melted away. The nerves reconnected and electric impulses moved freely again.

"We offer our humble appreciation for your healing. We welcome this Drakken to our fold, patient to see his true form, your soldier to command, welcomed guardians."

A hot wind blew over the assembly, and then the circle popped open with enough force to snap against their eardrums.

Carlisle came to with a groan.

Regina rushed to his side.

"I'm connected to a seriously pissed lizard." Carlisle groaned. "Can you help me up and stand back?"

She moved away as Ben and Max helped him to his feet.

"You might want to step back." They faced an orange dragon, similar but smaller in form than Mitch's great red Drakken.

"Very nice." Regina approached him, placing her hand on his

foreleg. "Wait until you're steadier before you begin flying. You can walk around here for a bit, get the feel of your new form."

"*Yes, Doc.*" His mental voice was strong and pleased.

Mitch stood back as the last of his team, the dragon force, the Drakken Brotherhood emerged from hell and took his first steps in freedom and security. His team complete, he would have to notify his boss they'd be ready for missions any time.

The Beginning
The Drakken Brotherhood

An Exciting Preview

James

Drakken Brotherhood
Book 2

Chapter 1

Tracy paced the floor, one hand raking through the tangled frizz of her blond hair, the other cradling her belly. She'd called Regina. She couldn't keep the secret any longer. The doctor and her best friend would know what to do, what advice to give.

Jimmy had awakened her this morning with a goodbye kiss. She'd smiled and yawned, pretending she still slept. He left happy and she'd gotten up. A hot shower later, she pulled a maternity dress over her head. The summer print that looked out of place in the middle of winter was comfortable, and she needed emotional support.

The knock on the door startled her out of her musings and pacing. She hurried over and opened the door. Seeing Regina's curious smile she broke into sobs and fell into her cold embrace.

"Honey, what is it? Let's get you inside, keep you warm." Regina pushed her into the house and closed winter out. In the mountains winter came early, but the men were still practicing together.

Regina was sure Mitch was looking carefully at mission orders to test his team, wanting to cherry pick the best one for the combined brotherhood.

"What's going on, Trace?" Regina dropped her coat on the foyer table and moved them into the living room, close to where flames crackled heat into the room. She loved watching the cheery warm fire. She pulled her friend down beside her on the couch and held her sweaty hands.

"I'm pregnant." Another round of sobs accompanied the confession.

Reggie smiled. "Yes, I know. I found out six months ago, when you told me." It was a dark time for Regina, and Tracy had tried to coax her back to happiness. "Calm down and tell me what happened? You're starting to worry me." She slid back, nestling into the cushions. "It isn't that stubborn husband of yours, is it? I can call Mitch and he'll beat the snot out of him in the ring today."

Tracy smiled, sniffled and shook her head. "Not Jimmy, exactly." She got to her feet again, as gracefully as a woman seven months pregnant could. Pacing, she again rubbed her belly.

"I'm all ears." Regina watched her, looking at her as a patient and not a dear friend. She'd gained weight, maybe a little more than she should. Her ankles weren't swollen, and her skin looked fresh and dewy, where it wasn't splotchy from crying.

"I don't know where to begin."

"Just start. When I have questions, we'll cover it then."

"I was afraid I'd lose Jimmy." Regina moved to the edge of the couch, tucking her feet under her and clasping her hands between her knees. She suddenly had a frisson of fear but curbed her impatience. She had to be wrong.

"I didn't want to live without him or worry that he'd be taken from me." Tracy stopped pacing and turned to face Reggie. "I started taking the serum after everything went to hell."

To her credit, Reggie didn't blink, she couldn't. Nor could she breathe. Goddess, damned. This was another chapter they didn't need written in the medical books. They hadn't found much of interest in the hours of notes collected on the military experiment, and nothing had involved a female, except Regina, who'd been taking it without her knowledge or consent. To have Tracy admit to entering into the trial on purpose?

"So what has been happening?"

"I'm not sure."

Regina got to her feet. "Grab a coat, we need a full workup and I want to see baby James." She followed her own orders and turned to wait on Tracy as she slipped her feet into boots.

"You're not yelling at me." Tracy slung the handle of her purse over her shoulder.

"Should I be?" Regina checked the lock and closed the door behind them. Flurries danced in the slight breeze, leftovers from the major storm. She helped Tracy into her car, and then she moved behind the wheel. "I have to admit it's a little late."

"I know." Tracy ran her hand through her hair, mussing the

untamed fuzzy mass even more,

"What were you thinking?" Regina moved quickly through the traffic, heading for her office. She'd applied for a license and opened a private practice. Appointments only and open three days a week. The other two days she worked on continuing to learn about the experiment and what happened to the men who'd participated in it and lived.

"When did you start?"

"When the dust settled, after we lost Mitch. I started a diary." Reaching into her purse, she pulled out a spiral notebook. The cover was tattered.

"How long did you take them?"

Silence filled the car until Regina wanted to shout. She gripped the steering wheel and turned into the drive to her office. She pulled in and parked, finally turning to look at Tracy.

"Until yesterday morning."

"Gods' balls." Regina got out of the car on the curse. Not waiting for Tracy, she turned off the alarm and locked the car as Tracy joined her on the covered porch.

About Carol Shaughnessy

Carol is a lifelong writer. Born in Vermont, she drifted south with her Navy husband until there was no snow to shovel. Now living in Georgia, she is lucky enough to be a full-time writer. She heads a local writer's support group and was nominated for a Ménage Award for her Sanctuary series. She writes paranormal fiction, because vampires, werewolves, and dragons are hot!

When not traveling, cruising or flying to far off countries, Carol hosts weekend fires around a large pit. There friends and family gather, new and old, for wine, laughs and s'mores.

Find Carol here:

www.facebook.com/pages/Sanctuary/194370797349137

www.amazon.com/Carol-Shaughnessy/e/B001r42BPI

Twitter: @carolssexytales

Instagram: carol_shaughnessy

Made in the USA
Middletown, DE
10 February 2021